JUST RIGHT

BY

TOM LEWELLEN

Acknowledgements

Here's what I truly love: getting up very early in the morning, and before I sit down to write, thanking God for my good fortune. My great fortune is not monetary. My opulence lay with the women in my life who have secured me, anchored me with good sense and emotional health, and allowed me the freedom to seek out ambitions from which many families would run.

I thank my two wonderful children McKenna and Hannah. No father could be prouder of the fine women they have become. It gives great comfort to know that I will leave the world a much better place when I depart. Soon they will take the helm of responsibility from my generation and the future could not be in better hands.

I thank my wife, my greatest gift. She is my best friend and lover, and prime mover and teacher for my children. She has taught them to be smart and good stewards of character and integrity. She has also been my constant supporter, especially with my political activities and writing. With not one political bone in her body, her continual support means very, very much to me.

And I thank the leader of this family of women, my wife's mother, Paula Hokanson. She is the inspiration of this book, not because of her politics, but because she is the very incarnation of a Great American. It should be the mission of our government, of any government, to understand how she built a great life for herself, her daughters and now continues to help build the next generation in her grandchildren. You will find out more about her under 'Paula the Great.'

Forward

The central strategy of this book is to stir debate. This is not a text book. There is no exacting political science or economic theory proposed that is right or wrong, or workable and efficient, or unworkable and inefficient. There is no exacting endpoint in Just Right. It is a journey.

The book is deliberately short to make a quick read for just about anyone from the average Joe who wonders what the 'heck' is going on in Washington to an economist or politician seeking a slightly different point of view.

The central theme of the book evaluates the differences between Leftist Democracy and Liberal Democracy. The author apologizes to the reader up front, as my primary motive is to re-establish the classic definition of Liberal Democracy. For those who have come to believe the Leftist Democracy and Liberal Democracy are the same, they are not. In fact, the pillars of Leftist Governance; strong central government, equality in all things, social and economic justice, and reason absent faith and in direct conflict with the pillars of Liberal Governance; individual liberty as the catalyst of greatness, decentralized power of government, hard work and faith with reason. (For more details on these styles of governance, I delve into this topic more deeply in *Irreconcilable Differences*.)

Liberalism is not only a belief in these pillars but execution of government using these pillars.

Just Right, then, is about the political notions that elect our leaders and the method and effectiveness of the tools of leadership. How big should government be? That is the debate. The most effective government will inevitably be smaller and more nimble than the Leviathan in Washington today.

Contents

INTRODUCTION

"I come too what my only serious criticism is," Maynard Keynes wrote to Friedrich von Hayek in 1922 regarding his thinking on the deficiencies of central planning and the management of the economy. 'You admit here and there that it is a question of knowing where to draw the line. You agree that the line has to be drawn somewhere; and that the logical extreme is not possible. But you give us no guidance whatever as to where to draw it.' (Keynes, Collected Writings Volume 17, 1920-2, Pages 285-7)

Keynes was both a towering presence and an immense intellect in the early 20th century. Keynes was a giant of a man at six feet six inches with charisma to match. In 1919, Keynes famously resigned his position as the English Treasury representative during the post-World War I negotiations with Germany. English negotiators went against his advice and imposed harsh reparations to be paid by German after the surrender in World War I. Keynes had warned the costly reparations would create a second war 20 years hence proved to be prescient.

Hayek, though a great intellect, did not have the personal charm of Keynes though he had a great impact on the conversation between Keynesian economics and the more traditional Austrian School of Economics. Hayek's great contribution to the argument, *The Road to Serfdom*, is a titanic and scathing book articulating the ineffective results of central planning. The book found a great readership in both Europe and America. These two great talents never initiated a formal debate of their policies and philosophy. The

Keynesian approach to monetarism and government intervention in economic policy was rapidly consumed by universities, rolling over the then aging notions of free-markets and the Austrian School of Economic theory. When Hayek was asked why Keynesian economics had been so thoroughly accepted by economists and politicians around the industrialized world, his slow and deliberate response came back as he thought economist like the 'control.' Indeed!

These two great economic minds would become Nobel Laureates in Economics. They drove heated debate via scholarly papers about how to achieve full employment as well as the deficiencies of centralization. Keynes believed government could borrow money (stimulate demand) and create government make-work jobs. Paychecks taxes for these workers, Keynes believed, would ripple through the economy creating a multiplying effect that would pay for the borrowing in new tax revenues. These money 'multipliers' are used by Keynesians today to value the effects of government 'stimulus.' Hayek, an Austrian, whose English was poor and writing difficult to read, lead the traditional economic faction in Europe. The scholarly deficiency of laissez-faire approach left economists without the technical tools provided by Keynesians for economists to rule the economic roost. The 'invisible hand' was not quite to interesting as the new science of econometrics generated by Keynesian thinking.

Neither Keynes nor Hayek would ever draw the line concerning how much central planning is too much nor how much is too little. Keynes won the popular vote among aspiring economists, then and since. As a result today's Keynesian economists and politicians have provided an open road for Western governments' central planning and a blank check to borrow and spend at will. In Keynes' early life, his full-employment theory was not well-received by the English political leadership during the '20s. In America, during the '30s his calculus was readily employed by FDR and his Brain Trust. The results of stimulus spending, though, never really returned the expected payback for Keynes' demand side solution. After six years of excessive federal spending (stimulus), even FDR's Secretary of

Treasury Henry Morgenthau said that the spending was not working, that something else needed to be tried. Though Keynesian methods have been tried repeatedly by both Republicans and Democrats since FDR, scant results from Keynesian stimuli have never stopped politicians from deficit spending. And so the borrowing and spending have continued for decades, accelerating to annual trillion dollar borrowing blitzes under the Obama administration.

The 'logical extreme' of which Hayek speaks - how far does the spending and borrowing ascend before the bottom drops out of the economy?   We are there. The tipping point where debt burdens debilitate potential economic growth is here.

The question remains, at what point does government centralization of power through increased taxation and/or deficit spending initiate the slide from our current tepid economic recovery to a dive over the financial cliff. Alternately, what government size is essential to *great* economic results? At what level does our society and culture flourish?   How much government is too much? How much is too little? To this end, I believe Goldilocks may be the girl who brings adoring economists to her feet. Yep, Goldilocks. She is the heroine of 'Just Right.' She has the wisdom of ages to determine what Just Right is.

Goldilocks' intrusion into the Three Bears home was not the work of a meddling political philosopher. Her breaking-and-entering though does give insight into the mission of this book: discovering best practices for our elected officials and bureaucrats in Washington. Like Goldi our leaders should try her process: - test-result, test-result, test-result: Just Right.

> *There on the kitchen table were three bowls of porridge.*
> *Goldilocks was hungry so she took a bite from the large bowl of porridge, but it was too hot.*
> *Then she tried the middle-size bowl, but it was too cold.*
> *Then she tried the smallest bowl, and it was just right, so she ate it all up.*

Aristotle, Roger Bacon, and Galileo were the forefathers of Goldi's thinking. These great minds brought the scientific method to bear and mankind prospered. Though science, discovery, and experimentation were largely lost in the Western world for nearly two millennia after Aristotle, Bacon, Galileo, and horde of experimental scientists in the 17th and 18th centuries provided an intelligent onramp for technology and innovation that propelled economic growth in England, Europe and America.

When applying the scientific method to political and social science, Goldi's methods did not fare so well mostly because the science was political. Marx and a litany of his philosophical progeny followed communism with a multitude of flavors of scientific socialism. These theories turned out to be neither scientific nor did they produce great social results. Political policy based on socialism, Progressivism, Statism and communism though indeed about experimentation, were never about understanding results of a social hypothesis. Results were secondary to ideology, and acquisition of power transcended ideology.

Theory without proof for modern political science parallels the not so scientific approach of Kings and Pontiffs during the Dark Ages. No proof was needed that the Earth was the center of the universe. The Church said it was so, so it was true. Galileo had proof that the earth revolved around the sun, but religion trumped science, as did as did politics. Galileo spent nine years in jail for stating his beliefs.

Today, circumstances have changed. Naysayers do not go to jail in the West. They are ignored or called names. The anti-Keynesian, Ronald Reagan, who adopted Milton Friedman's liberal economic policies, had his solutions branded 'Voodoo Economics.' George W. Bush was stupid and a liar. If you disagree with Global Warming science, you are a part of the Flat Earth Society. The Left pilloried Paul Ryan for daring to reform Medicare saying his solution would send granny, in her wheel chair, over a cliff. No jail, just a never ending verbal barrage for daring to suggest change. Even science has been the butt end of not so scientific bludgeoning for proposing ideas not coveted by the politics of correctness. Dr. Leo

4

Gomez, a former nuclear scientist said 'Religion is available to both the Left and the Right, with equal fervor. ... People with religion accept anything told to them by their heroes and don't feel the need to verify any of them.' (Cravens, 2007, 113-114) By religion, Dr. Gomez alluded to science without proof. His incredulity surrounds the political *science* surrounding the safety of the nuclear industry, by every scientific standard, the safest energy industry on the planet. The industry endures constant harangue from the left that creates false fear, uncertainty and doubt for which there is little escape back to reality.

Without verification of results of any theory of governance or economics, Just Right is impossible. Without setting specific objectives for what great results should be, governance becomes a sham of spin and propaganda.

Since Woodrow Wilson's presidency, which initiated the federal government's rapid expansion in the twentieth century, and included creation of the income tax, the Federal Reserve and the Federal Trade Commission, our federal government has expanded its roles and responsibilities in the name of change and experimentation. After Wilson came FDR's Social Security and another litany of government three letter agencies. Thirty years later LBJ's enacted Medicaid and Medicare. Bush added Prescription benefits to seniors and Obama the Affordable Care Act. Much government policy and many programs were *tested* over these last ten decades but few had any requirement for measuring results to assure quality or long term affordability. If metrics were set, they were summarily ignored or taxes adjusted upward as financial goals were missed. When Obama's stimulus assurances that unemployment would not rise past 8% but went over 10%, poor results were masked as the problem was bigger than 'we thought.' A bigger stimulus must have been required! So much for the economic science of money multipliers and econometrics. Few Democrats questioned the validity of Keynesian economic principle that government spending, even when borrowed, would create demand. Republicans did, but with little effect on policy. Keynesian policy still reigns king in the Obama administration despite poor outcomes.

Whatever government experiment that has been attempted over the last century and then failed to meet objectives, no transformations or major changes were proposed. Ultimately programs remained and then ossified into our government's immutable structure. Government policy was anti-Goldi. Test, ignore result; test ignore result; raise taxes to cover shortfalls.

It is hard to imagine a more devastating *worst* practice.

Unlike government, every American, *every human* – even our dear, fictitious Goldilocks, evaluates options then decides what works best. Failure creates new tests. Success seeks additional success. Unlike the Catholic Church's judgment of Galileo, where defense of orthodoxy is more important than fact or truth, success depends on measuring results and using results to improve our human condition.

Goldilocks' best practice for evaluation of life's little challenges was simple: test-result, test-result, test-result, decision. Her process worked so perfectly on the porridge; she used it as a best practice on the beds as well. She was on to something. It's important to test ideas to see if they produce good or bad results. Though she tested only porridge and beds, best practices are a great idea for just about everything we do in life. We all want great results in the things we do, the products we buy, the people with whom we have relationships, and even the people we elect to office. We are looking for Great. It's the American Way. Our decisions about what works best are meant to improve our condition, to find the right fit, to find what is *Just Right* for our lives. If what we choose does not produce good results, we change. We find a better solution.

Business operates under the same principle. CEOs and CFOs spend much time and money to assure best practices for business processes. Optimizing Order-to-Cash or streamlining manufacturing has huge payback in profitability and quality. In the 1950s Edward Deming, the Father of Continuous Improvement Process, took his new ideas about quality and process improvement for manufacturing to Japan after WWII. Japanese car makers after two decades of continuous improvement broke into the American car market with solutions that were significantly better than our Chevys, Chryslers and Fords. It took three decades for the Big Three to catch up, but like all successful businesses, declining market share, competitive fire, and poor profits drove each company to discover better business behavior, better design and better quality. What was 'Just Right' for the Big Three during the Fifties and Sixties was not a good barometer for what would be required for success in the '70s and beyond. The bar for 'Just Right' moved.

The same is true for government. The bar has moved. Solutions that were affordable, perhaps even sensible in the '30s, '40s and '50s, are breaking our bank today. Our ability to compete internationally is a function of the size and efficiency of our government and its oversight of our economy, our culture, and our society. Our government is growing in size and responsibility. It is also growing out of the control of the people we have elected to manage it. Much of our spending is on autopilot, the expenditures not even voted on, including big budget items like Social Security and Medicare and a variety of social welfare programs. The centralization of large power structures, especially political parties, whose only purpose is to assure the status quo has killed any opportunity to reform or transform government. As government grows, our personal options are slightly then severely limited. Creative political destruction is impossible because so much money is invested to assure nothing changes. American government is a $4 trillion enterprise, a size that is so great it has become an unmanageable Leviathan. It is a heavy weight that is difficult for our economy and society to bear.

Government is a tax on our productivity. The cost of government, like everything a citizen pays for, is only valuable if it is effective and affordable and if it helps our nation become more competitive in an increasingly competitive world. If the cost of government reduces our capacity to pay our bills, it reduces our capacity to compete. It narrows our road to success both personally, corporately and nationally. There is a point at which this tax on our productivity crimps economic growth and personal freedoms. America is at a tipping point where, without change, the real and crushing financial cliff of unfunded social program mandates will crush our greatness.

As important, this tax on our productivity can be too little or too great. Too little government causes anarchy and chaos. Too much starves our nation's productivity, innovation, and growth. For long term success, government cannot be too big or too small, not too controlling or too flexible, not too expensive or too cheap. 'Just Right' isn't one size nor a one-time event. It's a process. The process is not unlike Deming's Continual Improvement Process. It works when the worker and the leader communicate clearly and both understand the objectives and mission of the business. Government should work the same, but it doesn't. The voter has no set of clear objectives for governance. Without any guidance about how to reasonably size our government, voters will easily assume that any government is affordable as long as they can pay their bills, or, worse, as long as the government sends voters their federal dole each month whether in the form of a debit card of a business tax credit.

After the 2012 election a few of my Left leaning friends and Obama voters explained the president won their vote because the economy was doing fine and unemployment was improving and that overall things looked 'pretty good.' Really! This perspective was a bit shocking. Obama *should* be given credit but for great marketing, not for being a good president with a record of good results. Selling two percent economic growth and high employment as a reasonable achievement for re-election is not an easy thing to do, but the President managed. Goldie would not have found this 'bed' Just Right. These results are a bit soft.

Voters, though, do know something is wrong, but not what. Is eight percent unemployment satisfactory? Is 2% growth in GDP even mediocre? Is it possible that government spending at nearly 25% of GDP is economically unhealthy and an annual borrowing of $1 trillion harmful? Over the last three years Rasmussen polled Americans regarding 'Right Track, Wrong Direction,' and seldom have less than 60% felt America is on the right path. (Rasmiussen Reports, 2013) For 40%, life is good or good enough. Perhaps for voters who were too young to vote for Reagan or Clinton, Obama's results appear satisfactory enough for another four year. For older voters, perhaps Obama's weak results were satisfactory only because most have not been hurt. Their Social Security check comes every week. Their stocks are doing well. Christmas was merry.   Though something felt amiss there were no alternatives presented by Republicans to suggest they had a path to something more compelling.

The citizens who are harmed most by today's economic malaise are those at the bottom of the economic ladder and those who cannot yet vote, our children. Unemployment for minorities has skyrocketed during this recession. For those on the bottom economic rung economic opportunity has waned. Average American incomes have fallen. Perhaps government non-performance for the poor has become acceptable as income redistribution has increased.   For our children, though, the economic weight that is about to befall our next generation is fully uncontemplated.   They are two young to understand the consequences of a poorly performing government.

For the rest of us America headed in the wrong direction. The specific problem is not easily identified.   The spending.   Lack of leadership. Corruption. Debt. Surely, all of these are contributors to America's slow decent into mediocrity. But there is something more central to these issues, a root cause. Certainly spending and debt and lack of leadership are problems, but they are symptoms of something great issue.   These symptoms lead Americans to believe that government isn't on the right track.   They also are reason behind Congress' barely double digit approval rating. The last two presidents have seen their approval rating percentage drop into the low 40s. Something is wrong. Something is not 'Just Right.'

So what is the problem?   Our leaders have given up on Federalism and Liberal Democracy and, over the last 100 years, gravitated toward Leftist principles of governance. Our leaders have tossed aside the notion that our Nation's greatness begins with its people. Government has become the dispenser of debit cards and tax credits instead of the protectors of our freedoms and the enablers of our greatness.

The purpose of this book is to articulate the challenges of two of America's three adventures into constitutional government. The first section delineates the deficiencies of the slide toward a Living Constitution, toward a Leftist Democracy whose lineage began with Woodrow Wilson, gained legal standing with FDR and broke much further left with LBJ and Obama. The second section articulates the strengths federalism and Liberal Democracy. The objective is to discover which style of government is best, which fits our needs best and what is *Just Right* for creating the American Dream.

The Articles of Confederation, the first of America's three Constitutional journeys, will not be a topic of 'Just Right' as it should be apparent that our nascent nation discovered after the Revolutionary War that the Articles were too weak. They were designed to assure the power and responsibilities of the central government did not overshadow those of the states. The document, only six pages long, did maximize the strength of the states over a central authority to the exclusion of making a cohesive republic. The Articles had no ability to lay and collect taxes. They did provide the power to make war, to proclaim independence, and ultimately through a series of tragic defeats and a single crucial win at Yorktown, the defeat of the British Empire. But it did not build a nation, only a loose collection of states. The colonies that had formed in the 17th and 18th centuries held the political power based on history, experience and longevity. Giving up sovereignty to create a strong central authority, even to fight the most important war in the history of the world, had no political legs. The 'too little' government of Articles of Confederation gave way to the Constitutional Convention where 'Just Right' was the topic of conversation every day.

From the end of the Revolutionary War until James Madison began to organize the Constitutional Convention as the lack of depth of the Articles of Confederation made fundamental governance for any central authority very difficult. Having neither the ability to coin money nor mechanisms for trade between the states and other nations prevented America from coalescing into a single people. Without the ability to lay and collect taxes, the ability to build an Army and Navy to defend America was all but impossible. With no center, there was no nation. Yet most legislators and citizens across the various states believed a strong central government would sap not only the power of the states but the liberties of their citizens as well. The harrowing years of war with England, fought so hard and with such loss of life to win the liberties Americans so enjoyed would not easily be given away to a central authority.

As the delegates convened for the constitutional convention, many shared Ben Franklin's attitude. He said he 'smelled a rat,' worrying that the call for a new constitution would dissolve the powers of the states. Though the smelly rat may have hung over the convention and indeed reigned in the very few who sought a much stronger national government, the realty of the convention fell to the organizational magnificence of Federalism, a central government balanced by the power of the states and the liberties their citizens.

It is highly probable that every delegate understood two key notions for the ultimate success of the social contract they produced: 1) individual liberty was the catalyst for economic, social and cultural greatness, and 2) too little government, as well as too much government, was the enemy of liberty and a counterweight to America's potential greatness.

What they probably could have never guessed was that the decentralized structure they designed would also become the enlightened organizational structure of modern businesses over two hundred years later. Great businesses today mimic our federal approach, moving goals and responsibilities to regions and locales, empowering individuals on the shop floor or at the retail store cashier to make moment to moment decisions about quality and customer service. Old, centralized companies, with towering organizational charts and hardened chains of command that made decision making difficult if not impossible (think the old GM and Kodak) have been replaced by flatter more nimble corporations, like Google, Whole Foods, and Intel.

After 236 years, as companies are trying to flatten their organizations and empower their employees, our government has moved in the opposite direction, toward more centralization, experimenting with giant government monopolies and mandates that retard progress and become self-fulfilling prophecies of bigger and bigger government, towards a Leftist, European Democracy.

The question that should be answered is whether the Leftist direction is a solution that will keep American on a perpetual road to greatness, or whether something slimmed down, more nimble, with smaller budgets and less power, a Liberal Democracy based on Federalism, is a better direction?

Goldilocks' test/result methodology is only part of a larger equation for optimizing government, but a deeper dive into Liberal and Leftist cultures of governance is required. Both the 'Deficiencies of the Left' and 'Efficiencies of Liberal Federalism' are defined not as a proof of which is better but an instruction of how to define what level of each may be required for national success. The larger purpose of the book is to create debate between economists, politicians and voters. The voters are in a knowledge vacuum caused by an avalanche of political platitudes backed by hundreds of millions of dollars of advertising. Little in the way of practical intelligence is communicated. Without substantive debate about Leftist and Liberal Democracy, about Keynesian and traditional economics, about what defines American exceptionalism, voting becomes more about assuring the status quo and not about solving America's problems.

Just Right is a starting point as much as journey. There's lots of porridge to be tested.

THE ROLE OF GOVERNMENT

There has never been a political philosopher whose mission it was to create mediocre or poor social contract upon which a nation would be built. Even dictators seek to build a great nation, if only to satisfy their own selfish interests. Listen to nemesis of Capitalism, Karl Marx. He opens the 'Communist Manifesto,' stating his goal for a classless society.

> 'The history of all hitherto existing societies is the history of class struggles. Freeman and slave, patrician and plebeian, lord and serf, guild-master and journeyman, in a word, oppressor and oppressed, stood in constant opposition to one another, carried on an uninterrupted, now hidden, now open fight, a fight that each time ended, either in a revolutionary re-constitution of society at large, or in the common ruin of the contending classes.' (Marx, 2005)

Marx warred against class oppressors and for a classless society. He believed that Communism would not only create a great society, but a perfect society, a perfect world. Though his theories have no of constructive results or positive national outcomes, surely his purpose was to create a great society.

The 18th, 19th and 20th centuries are filled fill notions and theories about how to perfect man, society, and government. From the Left, and following in the footsteps of Marx, were Engels, Lassalle, Fourier, and in America, Dewey, La Follete, Croly, and a litany of others. Each had a vision of Leftist ideology that they believed would create a perfect society. Today's social engineers are part of a long political lineage that started with the French Revolution, transitioned from Marx and ends with our Leftist tilt that began early last century and has been rapidly accelerated this century with Bush and Obama. The Left's began with the French Revolution and it's philosophical father Jean Jacques Rousseau and energized into action by Robespierre. Robespierre's political progeny who followed his ideas of terror were Lenin, Mao, Pot Pol and Castro. The softer side of the Left flourished in 20th Century in Europe and found alignment in the Democrat Party with Woodrow Wilson, FDR, and LBJ.

Were any of these famed authors and leaders hoping to create a Dystopia? Not one.

The advice Marx gives before launching into the above elocution is something that all politicians should remember: 'It is high time that Communists should openly, in the face of the whole world, publish their views, their aims, their tendencies, and meet this nursery tale of the specter of Communism with a Manifesto of the party itself.' Wouldn't it be nice if our politicians would publically air their core beliefs, aims and tendencies so we could figure out for whom and what we are actually voting? Marx actually believed what he published. For our current politicians speaking their true feeling is considered a gaff of major political proportions.

When Obama told Joe the Plumber that he just wanted to 'spread the wealth around,' a flood of political second guessers leapt into the blogosphere condemning the Socialist comment. The candidate immediately distanced himself from his own comment though it was apparent he believed precisely what he said. No debate between candidates ensued. The opportunity to clarify or debate his position was lost. In the mainstream media, Obama's comments rang more about taxes than social theory and Obama's Leftist tendencies were masked.

When Joe Biden recommended that "We need to spend so we don't go broke,' no mention was made that this odd comment is a derivative of Keynesian economics. But the citation should go to Keynes, as he is the primogeniture of this kind of thinking. Romney's statement that 'There are 47 percent of the people who will vote for the president no matter what,' referring to the 47% of people who do not pay taxes, was portrayed as a major mistake, but, in fact, 47% of citizens do not pay Federal taxes. (Bingham, 2012) Even the Left should consider that paying no taxes is an inequitable solution. Just when the discussion should have gotten serious, debate was erased, replaced by ad hominem attacks from Left and Right. Both Biden and

Romney were reviled by opponents. No debate about spending or taxation resulted from either comment.

This is the politics of the mundane. Any meaningful discussion of our problems is transformed into a set of glittering generalities. The role of government is seldom, if ever, discussed. But ask any politician their intent: 'to build a greater America' is their answer. To support the middle class. To create jobs. But tying the objective to a plan is not part of anyone's leadership package. A politician's plan is to get elected, and stay elected. Our government is a government built to make the powerful more powerful and the rest of us second class citizens. We have replaced Liberalism with a set of lesser ideas that feature and exalt a powerful government that serves its own selfish interests. In this audacious adventure, the gamers in Washington have managed to deface the motion of Liberal governance by naming big government initiatives Liberal. To set the record straight there is nothing Liberal about big government, about intrusive government, or controlling government. Nothing!

Liberalism is about giving the individual choices, about increasing the power an individual wields in their lives, about individual greatness measured in the millions of citizens, not a few.

On the liberal side of history John Locke, Adam Smith, Montesquieu, Jefferson, and Madison created the theses of notions about freedom that gave us two very unlikely Presidents that executed on forming a smaller less intrusive government; Reagan and Clinton.

For the Left, history provided Rousseau's 'General Will', trumped Marx's dictatorship of the Proletariat and Keynes theory that full employment could be achieve through government borrowing and spending. In America the confluence of these notions of much larger roles for government lead to the intrusive administrations of Wilson, FDR, LBJ and Obama.

Regardless of the author, political philosopher, or political instigator, every player mentioned above sought greatness as a minimum result for their ideas. Solving problems to the best of our ability is part of our humanity whether we are Karl Marx or James

Madison, Osama bin Laden or William Wilberforce, Maynard Keynes or Friedrich von Hayek. Problem-solving is at the core of our humanity and humans are masterful at it. Take away all of our problems and leave us with nothing to solve and we transform into a group of simians looking for food and a desire to be preened by our mate. In perfect world our problems will never be fully extinguished. We will always have something to discern, to postulate about, to hypothesize - to understand and fix. Problem-solving is at the root of finding greatness. So the question, then, for the reader and for the author to answer is what are the elements of greatness upon which our nation should be built? What are the tools with which to best solve our problems? Upon the classless society of Marx? Upon individual liberty and rule of law as part of a long English and American tradition? Upon the French Revolution's motto 'Liberty, Fraternity and Equality?' On Liberal of Leftist notions of governance?

Are America's government and our individual success a result of a government of the people by the people and for the people? Or, as our leftist brethren believe, is our greatness a derivative of the state, by the state and for the state? Were the answer obvious to every citizen, Just Right would be a valueless endeavor. The answer, though, is not even remotely obvious for any of the Western democracies. In America with the richest and deepest of Liberal traditions, about half of Americans have shifted to favor a state driven model of governance, while the other half favors the road less traveled, a liberal democracy driven by individual liberty and individual success.

Before Marx's blitzkrieg to annihilate the war between the classes, and Keynes economic model that government can borrow without limit, our founding fathers had a much different view of the purpose of government. The Preamble to the Constitution articulates the design of a highly focused government with limited responsibilities. The words are simple and do not lecture.

'We the People of the United States, in Order to form a more perfect Union, establish Justice, insure domestic

Tranquility, provide for the common defence promote the general Welfare, and secure the Blessings of Liberty to ourselves and our Posterity, do ordain and establish this Constitution for the United States of America.'

The Preamble to the Constitution summarizes the thoughts of our founding fathers' effort from 1787 to 1789. A Liberal will read the objectives of the Constitution in the Preamble to be very targeted on secure the blessings of liberty in perpetuity and a more perfect union a phrase about the weakness of the Articles of Confederation. The Left has an altogether different read. Promoting the general welfare has become the bell weather for using the full force of the government to implement a variety of social monopolies and establish justice has taken on the modifiers 'economic' and 'social,' which are in severe conflict with securing the Blessing of Liberty. But the greatness of the finished product, regardless of how it is ready, is monumental.

Ben Franklin noted, "When you assemble a number of men to have the advantage over their joint wisdom, you inevitably assemble with those men, all their prejudices, their passions, their errors of opinion, their local interests, and their selfish views. From such an assembly can a perfect production be expected? It therefore astonishes me, Sir, to find this system approaching so near to perfection as it does." (Franklin, 1787)

The document is indeed spectacular in its clean, simple language. It is the model of how legislation should be written. Only one other document exceeds the perfection of the Constitution, the Bill of Rights. Its language, unlike our modern Congressional language, is terse, directed and, frankly, downright beautiful. Conversely, our modern Congress' erudition and obfuscation in the form of Dodd-Frank, Obamacare or Sarbanes-Oxley would be the antonym.

Prior to the writing of the Constitution, Jefferson penned another brilliant document, the Declaration of Independence. He expressed the terms upon which American Government existed, from the consent of the governed.

> 'We hold these truths to be self-evident, that all men are created equal, that they are endowed by their Creator with certain unalienable Rights, that among these are Life, Liberty and the pursuit of Happiness.'
> That to secure these rights, Governments are instituted among Men, deriving their just powers from the consent of the governed, That whenever any Form of Government becomes destructive of these ends, it is the Right of the People to alter or to abolish it, and to institute new Government, laying its foundation on such principles and organizing its powers in such form, as to them shall seem most likely to affect their Safety and Happiness. Prudence, indeed, will dictate that Governments long established should not be changed for light and transient causes; and accordingly all experience hath shewn, that mankind are more disposed to suffer, while evils are sufferable, than to right themselves by abolishing the forms to which they are accustomed. But when a long train of abuses and usurpations, pursuing invariably the same Object evinces a design to reduce them under absolute Despotism, it is their right, it is their duty, to throw off such Government, and to provide new Guards for their future security.'

As one young co-worker stated to me upon his first reading of the Preamble to the Declaration, 'These guys were pretty serious, dudes.' Indeed they were. The Signers' endeavors in Philadelphia melded millennia of the thoughts and events and styles and manners of governments to mold a social contract that has withstood the test of time, competition, and endless withering assaults from monarchs, dictators, socialist tyrants and even America's elitist political class.

Our greatest challenges to Liberal thinking have been from within. Khrushchev's 'We will bury you', seems audacious but trifling compared to Woodrow Wilson's 'a lot of nonsense has been talked about the inalienable rights of the individual.' (Wilson, Constitution Government in the United States, 1908) Is it really possible a President of the United States would dare rattle the intellectual foundation of Liberalism? Sadly, yes. Actions, though, speak louder than words. Obamacare now mandates each of us to buy health insurance under threat of severe penalty. Is it reasonable for a President support the notion of Forced Action by the government? The idea is both anti-intellectual and also anti-liberal. FDR's threat court packing unnerved the Supreme Court's distaste for Social Security's constitutionality. Would the leader of the free nations of the world really wield power in such a way? A Leftist, yes. A Liberal, never.

President Wilson was the first in a long line of Presidents seeking to redraw the power structure architected by the Constitution. "The Constitution was not made to fit us like a straightjacket. In its elasticity lies its chief greatness." (Wilson, 20th Century Quotes on Constitutional Liimits, 1904) What Wilson viewed regarding the flexibility of the Constitution is a far cry from the intent of Jefferson, Madison and crew in Philadelphia. Wilson, FDR, LBJ, and Obama weren't testing the flexibility of the Constitution to assure the rights of men, but to assure a well-ordered collective. Their role for government diverges from the well-articulated message of the Constitution and from any understanding of Liberal governance.

'Life, liberty and the Pursuit of Happiness,' in an earlier version of the Declaration read 'Life, Liberty and Property.' John Locke, one of the founding fathers' of modern, liberal governance and a favorite of many of the Founding Fathers coined this phrase a bit differently. From *Two Treatises of Government*:

> Sect. 87. 'Man being born, as has been proved, with a title to perfect freedom, and an uncontrouled enjoyment of all the rights and privileges of the law of nature, equally with any other man, or number of men

19

in the world, hath by nature a power, not only to preserve his property, that is, his life, liberty and estate, against the injuries and attempts of other men; but to judge of, and punish the breaches of that law in others, as he is persuaded the offence deserves, even with death itself, in crimes where the heinousness of the fact, in his opinion, requires it.' (Locke, Second Treatise of Government, 1690)

It is easy to understand why The Two Treatises of Government was so well read in the 18th Century. Locke draws from our common notions and beliefs to explain two important principles in the Declaration of Independence. First, that our most basic rights come from nature (and from God) and that these rights are the same for each of us. Second, these include life, liberty and estate, and our single most personal economic right: property - the most important property, our bodies, ourselves.

Leftist Democrats also believe that the basic fundamentals of a Liberal republic coupled with market capitalism may create wealth, but it does nothing for the spiritual side of man; that capitalism does not a better man make. Jefferson, though, stated that one of America's crucial aims is the pursuit of happiness, and that through property (our bodies) some degree of earned success results from our labor, for our own good. It is the hard work of our own labor that does provide a path to spiritual potential.

For John Calvin, the primogenitor of Calvinism, hard work was an essential requirement for entrance into heaven. 'There is no work, however vile or sordid, that does not glisten before God.' Hard work is an essential ingredient in the Protestant Work Ethic proposed by Max Weber in the 19th Century and a key component of the expansion of wealth in Europe. Capitalism and Liberal Democracy go hand in glove providing elements for both economic and spiritual success.

There is one more hint of what the Founding Fathers intentions were for the United States. This from Jefferson's Inaugural Address in 1801 and his Collected Writings:

20

'What more is necessary to make us a happy and a prosperous people? Still one thing more, fellow citizens -- a wise and frugal Government, which shall restrain men from injuring one another, shall leave them otherwise free to regulate their own pursuits of industry and improvement, and shall not take from the mouth of labor the bread it has earned" and, "If we can prevent government from wasting the labors of the people, under the pretense of caring for them, they must become happy.' (Jefferson, 1743 – 1826)

Would it be possible that a modern politician say such meaningful words? One could only hope. This is, in fact, the precise definition of 'Just Right.'

Government is a burden on our productivity. There is nothing worse than to execute your labor perfectly and have its value reduced by the weight of an inefficient and ineffective government.

Having great intentions about great governance is never so important as producing great results. Just Right's next two sections will articulate, first, the heavy weight created on individuals by a government too large, too strong, and too powerful and, second, a different approach to a more nimble federal government with better tools to build policy, and better focus measuring the results of its endeavors.

The two competing philosophies in Washington can be reduced to the essential axiom of each side. The Left believes government can organize a more perfect society via the will of rational men of intelligence, that man is imperfect and requires central guidance by government.

The Liberal believes that by maximizing liberty, citizens will naturally rise to their own level of greatness producing a great society, culture and economy. Citizens need only a sensible and simple legal framework for effectively competing for opportunities.

Hayek warned against the former by stating the logical extension of the centralization is communism, which did not work. The Founding Fathers' own invention of the Articles found too little government led neither to anarchy nor a national civil society.

Keynes provided the path that Marx did not, a blank for government to borrow and spend without reason. The road to *Just Right* lay somewhere between.

THE DEFICIENCIES OF LEFTIST DEMOCRACY

The objective of this section is not to exhaustively detail the challenges of a Leftist government but to provide insights into the key deficiencies that have helped to create slow economic growth and help stagnant political debate and commentary. Central themes about the culture of large government and its dependence on inefficient monopolies which increase the power, scope and cost of government have created the greatest barriers to social and economic success. Other policy deficiencies like elevated complexity and objectives to reduce individual and corporate risk and failure will also be discussed.

Deficiency One: Culture of Governance

Every social contract, every constitution, is built on cultural principles of governance and these principles are built on basic beliefs about mankind, about the God of that society, and the millennia of cultural tradition absorbed and constructed by its citizens. For Leftist Democracies, these pillars are 1) Centralization of Power, 2) Equality or forced equality supplanting liberty, 3), Economic/Social Justice and 4) Rationalism without faith.

The Left's pillars of governance are in direct conflict with Liberal notions of federalism built on 1) Decentralization of power, 2) Liberty as the building block for personal greatness, 3) Hard work as the key economic, personal and spiritual building block, and 4) faith with reason.

These American Leftist pillars sprung from notions of Rousseau's General Will and Robespierre's execution of *General Will* in the French Revolution's Reign of Terror.

> 'If the driving force of popular government in peacetime is virtue, that of Popular government during a revolution is both virtue and terror: virtue, without which terror is destructive; terror, without which virtue is impotent. Terror is only justice that is prompt, severe, and inflexible; it is thus an emanation of virtue; it is less a distinct principle than a consequence of the general principle of democracy applied to the most pressing needs of the patrie.' (Robespierre M. , 1794)'
> (Robespierre M. , 1794)

In the 20th and 21st centuries, terror in the Western democracies has been replaced by 'fear, uncertainty and doubt' promoted by politicians who wish to be elected, but whether a softer terror of the modern leftist democracy, or the terror of the jihad, the results are the same. The mission of government is to align the will of the governed to the will of the governors.

Rousseau's desire to create a *great* society was to be rooted in the best of intentions (like most Leftist Philosophies). He famously wrote, 'Man is born free, and everywhere he is in chains,' and 'Liberty is not to be found in any form of government; she is in the heart of the free man; he bears her with him everywhere.' There is little doubt that he understood the excesses of government. What he did not have is a faith in individuals to self-organize their own freedoms effectively. He clarifies his philosophy, his discomfort with humanity in his notion of General Will.

> 'As soon as this multitude (i.e., the people) is so united in one body, it is impossible to offend against one of the members without attacking the body, and still more to offend against the body without the members

resenting it. Duty and interest therefore equally oblige the two contracting parties to give each other help; and the same men should seek to combine, in their double capacity, all the advantages dependent upon that capacity.' (Rousseau, 1762)

This roughly translates into 'if you're with us, great, otherwise you are the enemy.' The Left pilloried George Bush for his statement, and rightfully so, when talking about defeating terrorism, but their criticism was ironic. The left is quite good at ostracizing those outside Leftist thinking. Few Republicans will challenge the programs and policies, from Medicare to Social Security to Government schools for fear of being politically incorrect, outside the Left's notion of the General Will. '

Rousseau and Robespierre have their fingerprints on the philosophies of Marx, Engels and Lenin in their politics of class struggles. Their dislike of the power of monarchs and their cronies and capitalists are easy to understand. One person, the King or tyrant, made the rules and had most of the money. What was there to like about this political situation. During the industrial revolution, ninety percent of the property and wealth was held by the nobility in Europe. What's to like about this economic structure? Replacing one tyranny, kings and tyrants, though, with the 'General Will' of the revolutionary mob is replacing one tyranny with another, if only with a more popular face. Lenin and Trotsky did exactly this in Russia. Mao did the same in China, and Castro duplicated the same in Cuba.

The problem with each Leftist revolution can be summed up by Rousseau's belief of 'forcing men to be free.' Individuals need to be told what to do so they can be happy, which ultimately means they conform to some notion of General Will defined by the Revolutionary Council. This view of man by the Left is the opposite of Liberal notions of man.

When Rousseau and Marx and America's Progressive brand of Socialism fell out of favor in America in the 1920's, the American Left renamed itself, changing the name Left to Liberal, which rang more of 1984's trilogy of Newspeak. 'War is Peace, Freedom is Slavery, and Ignorance is Strength.' Leftist is Liberal. Not really.

But the new branding still had the same negative underpinning of 'General Will' and a less than positive requirement for government to drive social engineering, individual intent. Maynard Keynes says this about the pedestrian citizen:

> 'It is not a correct deduction from the Principles of Economics that enlightened self-interest always operates in the public interest. Nor is it true that self-interest generally is enlightened; more often individuals acting separately to promote their own ends are too ignorant or too weak to attain even these. Experience does not show that individuals, when they make up a social unit, are always less clear sighted than when they act separately.'

This abject thinking is not new. This point of view can be traced back not only to Rousseau and the General Will, but to Kings and Queens over the millennia.

> 'Quite unexpectedly to almost all who watched the marketplace, many — though by no means all — ordinary men and women responded positively to new opportunities. This demonstration of a capacity to think for themselves and act in the own interests surprised their social superiors because it had long been assumed that simple farmers or small-town traders didn't possess the imagination to act outside

prescribed routines.' (Keynes, End of Laissez Faire, 1926)

That Kings and Queens consider subjects not able to take care of themselves, not able to think, is an extraordinary conceit carried into the present by the Left. The Left blithely suggest that they are just trying to help those in need of help, that person down the street, but that person down the street is looking up the street and thinking that you are the guy they are helping that needs help. In the end, we all live down the street, we all of need the guiding hand of the state. To be free, we must live inside the collective, the Village, the General Will.

In the 2012 State of the Union, President Obama squarely laid the location of our freedoms, "[W]e has always understood...that preserving our individual freedoms ultimately requires collective action." (Obama, Remarks by the President in the State of the Union, 2012) Though subtle, the underlying message is clear. Join the collective and we will all be free together. The reigns of freedom then belong to the collective, not you and your neighbor. Surely the Gestapo and KGB worked under the same thesis.

The Left's requirement for strong central government is not a 'Dictatorship of the Proletariat' but a vote for a soft tyranny that assures the ignorant do not take over, the ignorant being all citizens not part of those Progressives/Socialists/Statists elitist collective or General Will. The corollary of this requirement is that two classes of American's exist; you and I, the common citizens; and the Herbert Croly's *disinterested and intelligent* leaders we elect along with the bureaucrats they hire. By the Left's standards, this second class, the political class, is better fit to organize our General Will. The second class, the non-elites, is too ignorant, incompetent, or incapable to live our lives freely and need the wisdom of this first class. The political elite, as their power swells, tend to lead with *the not so gentle hand* of wisdom assuring the rest of us follow willingly. The Left sees social engineering as a bit like herding cats which is a bit of a challenge. So the gentle leftist wisdom generally becomes more onerous with time and requires a more military-like structure.

The preferred organization of American Leftist thinking is rooted in early Progressive thinking taken from Italian Fascists and is much like organizing for War. The Left organized the Peace Corps, the War on Poverty, the Civilian Conservation Corps, War Industries Board, and National Recovery Administration. The Left was the primogenitor of War-centric organizations, the Committee on Public Information, run by Progressives George Creel and Edward Bernays, who would be credited with creating the field of public relations and cut his teeth on the Creel Committee, learning the art of 'the conscious and intelligent manipulation of the organized habits and opinions of the masses.' (Goldberg, 2007) The leadership habits of the left tend toward military micro-managers who direct government with heavy-handed command and control systems to assure we cats walk in a straight line.

It should be no surprise to find Leftist government programs organize via a command and control structure based on a monopoly similar to the U.S. Military. Command and Control versus Lead and Manage is required because Americans are 'ignorant' and need to be 'manipulated' to succumb to the general will mandated by a litany of government monopolies. That is, to finally have only a single class of Americans, the *second class* need only be manipulated into 'enlightened' thinkers, willfully joining the club of enlightened Progressives and Leftists, or joining by force of law and/or mandates of a wise government.

The Left's two classes of citizens have led to two styles of governance, two cultures of governance. The Left proposes more controls, more power executed from the center in Washington. The Liberal solution, which has waned over the last century, understands the need to distribute power with Washington managing states and citizens to success.

Imagine a citizen, call him Joe, out of work, seeking employment in a down economy, who obtains an interview with two companies LeftCorp and Meracorp. Both companies have had

28

revenues drop 10% in the last year and have erected new business plans to get back on good financial footing. The hopeful job applicant lands a second interview with both companies with the CEO. No better situation could befall Joe. Each company must be very interested if the CEO is interviewing him.

At LeftCorp, the CEO is affable and genuine. He tells Joe that revenues were down, but they had a plan. LeftCorp had cut 10% of the dead weight from the sales staff and also cut wages among the staff which brought expenses in line with revenues. To increase revenues, the Executive VP of sales had completely rewritten the sales process. The CEO presents Joe with a thick 2000-page tome and plops it on the desk.

"A beauty, eh," the owner comments. "And... manufacturing we have done much the same. Floor workers have a manual on production specifics and a layer of management to assure perfect execution. To reduce costs on the line, we have reduced wages and brought on a new family less expensive of vendors from whom we will buy raw materials. We believe our cost of manufacture will drop 8% which gives us a price advantage over our competition. As important we have 82 different widgets on your product list to sell. A widget for anyone and everyone with a widget. Again, focusing on very low prices, we think everyone can own a widget."

"The sales plan lays out every conceivable question a customer might ask as well as the answer that goes with it. Additionally, we have completely rewritten the sales methodology which is described in the first 150 pages. This plan is a wonderful.' The CEO goes on to explain that an addition layer of senior sales managers have been added to assure that the sales plan is executed perfectly. For those whose have challenges retraining will be involved. "We believe with this plan every sales person will exceed their quotas. For those that do a small bonus will be awarded." After some discussion of Joe's stellar sales history, the CEO offers a Joe a job.

Joe's gets a slightly different view of a company, Meracorp that is also struggling to be profitable. "Joe," the CEO starts, "as you can imagine the economy is very tough right now. But we have a vision here at Meracorp that people want high-quality widgets and a good price and we are going to deliver that product to the market. You probably realize our revenues were off about 10% last year and we lost money. To get our income statement in order we did a couple of things. First, we went back to the engineers and asked for them to find ways that would streamline manufacturing to reduce costs and then asked purchasing to find better raw materials that would reduce rework and returns. Additionally, we have reduced everyone's pay by 5% and management is taking a 10% cut. But we want to pay this cut back to everyone in a success bonus. If we reach our revenue goal each month, everyone gets a 5% bonus. In sales, we streamlined our sales process to make it easier and so have been able to expand our manager's span of control from 7 sales persons to 9 reducing costs further.' The CEO holds up a single sheet of paper and says, 'This is the process. Simple and straightforward. There are only six steps in the sales process that we have tested over and over and they *just* work. We believe simplicity is the key, not only to sales, but design and manufacturing as well. The managers are just here to help when you get stuck or need help. They are here to help enable your success. Along with you commissions on sales, we have accelerated commissions past 100% of your objective because we want the incentives to help you accelerate past your personal goals and carry the company far past our company goals. To streamline your sales process even more we have reduced the number of widgets we sell from a family of 14 to 4 of our best sellers. And we are launching research and development for our newest widget, Widget 2.0."

Though there may be some who can't wait to work for Leftcorp and to have additional management to look over their shoulder and a 2000-page process to heel to, it is hard to imagine that number of people is high. It is also easy to imagine that the first company is going to have a very hard time meeting its revenue projections. Companies that have cheap products have only one lever to pull to win sales, cost. Low cost products of questionable value seldom are the foundation for a company with long term prospects.

What is different between the companies? Culture. One is built on a culture of success, the other one of control.

Reemphasizing the importance of culture in any organization, government or country cannot be understated. Our traditional culture of governance is built on a culture of success. It presumes citizens with a stable and simple legal structure will find their own level of success without government intervention. The Left's approach to government is based on control. Only with government intervention, either in the form of a personal check, burdensome regulation or a timely government tax credit, will society find greatness.

Liberal governance allows citizens the freedom to succeed or fail. Liberalism assumes failure is a natural part of success. In capitalism, failure is aligned with Joseph Schumpeter's concept of 'creative destruction.' 'The process of industrial mutation... incessantly revolutionizes the economic structure from within, incessantly destroying the old one, incessantly creating a new one...This process of Creative Destruction is the essential fact about Capitalism.' (Schumpeter, 1942) Though creative destruction is considered a theory pertinent business and industry, it is also part of our daily lives. When jobs are lost or investments tank, humans tend to redesign their thinking to restart their road back to success. It is only natural that humans would take this best practice and apply it to business they run.

Marx considered this destructiveness just one more problem with capitalism. For an ideologue dreaming of top-down management of an economy, this destructiveness seems divisive. For those with a bottom up approach, creative destruction, whether corporate or personal, is a healthy path toward a more efficient and effective solution.

The Left assumes failure is a typical human result which should be avoided and tries to overcome failure with extensive legislative oversight and social engineering that further inhibits success. Most Americans have worked for a micro-managed company like Leftcorp. Generally these companies are small because all decisions are driven up through management, many times to the owner or local executive, making decision-making time consuming and arduous. Growth is hamstrung because of the bottleneck at the boss' desk. Innovation is abated, if not annihilated by cumbersome business processes and unbending managers. As a small company grows from a mom and pop (if it can), the culture translates quickly into a command and control structure. Fear becomes the motivator for these organizations, fear of doing something wrong – 'if you blow this, you are fired.' This harkens back to Robespierre's notion of the need to lead with both virtue and terror. Though this type of business culture does occasionally succeed despite themselves, generally employee turnover is high.

In government, this culture stifles both business and individual initiative inside the organization but extends its inefficiencies to society at large. Our government increasingly micro-manages Americans. Where choice and simplicity reigned from the beginning of our nation through President Wilson, since his presidency one federal bureaucracy after another has sought some level of social engineering. FDR's restarted the onslaught of federal bureaucracies and welfare monopolies with Social Security In the sixties LBJ followed with Medicare, Medicare, the War on Poverty, The Great Society. Expansion of these programs ensued with Nixon and Carter. The only President to reign in any social monopoly (welfare was reconfigured to Workfare) was Clinton, an unwilling Republican in Democrat clothing. Rampant expansion followed with Bush's No Child Left Behind and Senior Prescription Drug Benefits and Obama tacked on the onerous program to date ObamaCare – with a very visible and market killing personal mandate to purchase health insurance. The largest and most enduring social monopoly with the most rigid three-tier government and union command and control monopoly that goes unnoticed is our $600 billion government education system. Like Leftcorp, these monopolies are not streamlining nor improving American society or culture.

Were the ideas of the Left effective, then each of these programs would either be financial sustainable, or because they did indeed build great Americans, the programs would inevitably shrink until they had no participants. Good social engineering should built successful citizens, not dependent citizens. The lists of clients in our government's social programs exceeds 80,000,000 today and is growing rapidly. The bills for these programs are unfunded to the tune of $106 trillion dollars over the next 30 years according to the CBO and Senator Ron Johnson (R) - Wisconsin. (Strong, 2013) Perhaps a bit of creative destruction might be a good idea.

Deficiency Two: Command and Control - and Enforce

One of the first lessons a soldier learns is that not obeying orders can get you shot from a bullet coming from a friendly gun after a very short military tribunal. Command and Control is an essential management structure for the execution of any war, any battle, and, for the Left, any political endeavor. The Air War College, a part of the United States Air Force and Air War College lays out the Command and Control message as this follows:

> 'In the broadest sense, command and control applies far beyond military forces and military operations. Any system comprising multiple, interacting elements, from societies to sports teams to any living organism, needs some form of command and control. Simply put, command and control in some form or another is essential to survival and success in any competitive or cooperative enterprise. Command and control is a fundamental requirement for life and growth, survival, and success for any system.' (Air War College, 2013)

Broad, indeed. Every organization needs some set of methods and processes to control logistics, administration, ordering, sales and planning, as well as leadership that may command these processes. For the military, the threat of death, fear, and a stint in the brig that gives leadership power. For business, the threat of firing or just a bad performance review is a kinder gentler threat, but a threat that helps assure some gauge of good business execution. The very nature and tenor of Command and Control also determines the culture of the organization. Like LeftCorp and Meracor, the personality of the company is determined by the personality of Command and Control, by the business culture and vision promulgated by the leadership. For LeftCorp, the daily aggravation of a manager looking over shoulders and continual readings of a 2000-page employee manual will inspire few workers to greatness while Meracor's command system is built around enabling success and the freedom of a simple business process for sales. The question isn't that there is a command and control system in every organization. The question is what culture does that system create? Is it something lean, easy to understand and which rewards greatness and provides paths away from mediocrity and failure? Or does the system assume coercion is required for success where there is little simplicity and few rewards for success and a high expectation of failure that should be avoided at all costs.

Leftist Government, perhaps because of the military approach adopted by Wilson and FDR, and their associated Progressive Brain Trusts that accompanied the development of so many government programs modeled after the military, has chosen the LeftCorp approach to social management. This approach has produced both monopolies for social policy formed with onerous mandates and bureaucracies to enforce heavy-handed regulatory and tax environments. Couple the government's need for control tied to a Lawyer's signature ability to articulate control in obscure legal language, further combined with an enormously bad habit for creating government monopolies and one has a nearly complete history of America's swing in the 20th century to the Left, away from economic and political liberalism.

Like almost every organization, with the passing of time, Government has had a concomitant growth in control, and with more control a parallel increase in power. In the corporate world businesses grow old and stodgy with increasingly complicated processes. With age some fail. Good businesses, great businesses, fight a continuous battle to allay this aging process. Many businesses that ignore the need to change fail. Most rethink their structure, refocus on their customers and remake their core business. For government, there is no profit motive, no reason to restructure. There is only a steady fare of public choice via rent-seeking elected officials who hope to increase political power. Washington's consumption of power has led America to a tipping point, moving from a liberal democracy to the tyranny we voted for, one that has and is leading to the a long, slow decline in economic results and potentially down the Road to Serfdom.

Rent-seeking is the foundation of Leftist thinking. The Left believes that they are a special class of leaders who, once elected, become disinterested public service savants that understand and promote the General Will. They believe the greed of capitalist has harmed citizens and that one of government's key requirements is to control this greed with regulation. Only with a disinterested public servant is able to control this greed. Nobel Laureate James Buchanan expressed quite a different theory, that politics and political programs had value, generally in exchange for money or power. Put another way: money seeks power both in business and government.

> 'If the government is empowered to grant monopoly rights or tariff protection to one group, at the expense of the general public or of designated losers, it follows that potential beneficiaries will compete for the prize. And since only one group can be rewarded, the resources invested by other groups-which could have been used to produce valued goods and services-are wasted. Given this basic insight, much of modern politics can be understood as rent-seeking activity. Pork-barrel politics is only the most obvious example. Much of the growth of the bureaucratic or regulatory sector of government can best be explained in terms of the competition between political agents for constituency support through the use of promises of discriminatory transfers of wealth.' (Buchanan, Politics Without Romance, Spring 2003)

Are their disinterested leaders that can really understand the optimum 'general will?' Are their central planners whose wisdoms will perfectly allocate resources?

36

According to Buchanan, probably not. There is no 'omniscient decision' maker to maximize 'social utility.' (Buchanan, Public Principles of Public Debt, 1999)

With each opportunity to spend our precious tax dollars a secondary process of power consumption is generated to foster further spending. More spending creates more power creates more spending. This is a deadly fiscal cycle now generates $2 trillion in annual spending on social policy that either intrudes in our freedoms masquerading as good intentions or policy that is designed to control our lives.

Government has stippled our society with small, but challenging intrusions into our personal lives. Most would consider this creeping micro-management small paper cuts and acceptable for the greater good, but Leftist control solutions are manifest at every level of government from local to federal, and across all branches of government – and continually growing.

Approaching retirement age our elders will discover that to enroll in Social Security one must enroll in Medicare. Must. This is a Clinton Administration mandate which when challenged by seniors, U.S. District Judge Rosemary Collyer found "no loophole or requirement that the Secretary provide such a pathway." That pathway is Social Security free of the Medicare requirement. Why? The why is simply not clear. Perhaps the government should also mandate that seniors must enroll for food stamps or the stamp of the month club from the post office.

ObamaCare mandates that the 17% of the population that does not wish to purchase very expensive HMO/PPO health insurance (another mandate foisted on us by Mr. Nixon) must indeed buy Obamacare or be fined (taxed, if your name is Justice Roberts.) Why? In this case, the Obama administration purports that by doing so the cost of healthcare will diminish for us all. Sadly, that seems not to be the case.

If you want to enroll your children in a different state-mandated, government monopoly school other than the one inside your district's designated borders in Ohio, beware, you may be on your way to jail. Kelley Williams-Bolar did just that. After suffering too long with schools that did not provide a quality education she enrolled her children in a neighboring district. After being sentenced to 10 days in county jail she noted, "I don't think they wanted money? They wanted me to be an example." A micro-managers dream - not only did she have to fight the government there was a judge at the ready to support the school's cause. Unlike a business, there is no HR or consumer affairs department to help out when sensible business processes might prevail. Government has no business processes or best practices, just a heavy hand. And Ms. Williams-Bolar's profession? Educator. Ironic.

Sarbanes-Oxley sprang from the terrible excesses of a few companies intentionally abusing accounting rules. To assure the few were punished, Sarbanes loaded up a truck full of additional accounting rules to assure the bad guys followed the rules – and the good guys too. The result: bad guys still are bad. The new rules didn't catch Bernie Madoff or Lehman Brothers. The legislation, though, brutalized the IPO market, reducing the number of companies going public since Sarbanes by one half. These smaller companies attempting to create a new capital stream via an IPO to fund growth find Sarbanes costs too high, preventing a public offering from being a reasonable return of value.

Government increasingly purports to aid the common good, but by treating the populace like ignorant masses they fall short. Try to buy a 100W light bulb; no can do. They use too much electricity says Congress. They do not exist. Ditto for top load washers – too much water. High-volume flushes for toilets exist only in the past so it is a two-flush society. Government invades our lives to protect us from … ourselves perhaps. For every attempt to micro-manage some facet of our lives or the economy an unintended consequence is created.

The Dodd-Frank legislation for financial reform bill was a slow, lengthy response to the financial meltdown of 2008. The meltdown occurred because of four factors, 1) relaxation of mortgage application rules to allow for more permissive process for loan application acceptance for low income mortgages (this occurred both during the Clinton and Bush presidencies), 2) rising desire of both Freddie Mac and Fannie Mae to purchase more loans in the housing market as part of their directive to assure high risk loans (and increase their power and revenues), 3) the allowance by the government for financial institutions to package mortgages together (losing transparency of value for individual mortgages, and 4) the Fed's policy of low interest, very low interest – i.e. cheap money looking for a home, so to speak. The 2000 page plus document, plus the yet to be finished hundreds of pages surrounding the Volker Rule have little or nothing to do with the central problem, lack of simple, effective government oversight in two areas: a reasonable loan application qualification process and focus by the Fed on cheap money causing bubbles (like the one forming in 2012-3 in the stock market from cheap money and Quantitative Easing.)

After the meltdown, the loan industry self-corrected and fixed the loan application problem, though belatedly Frank-Dodd does have some guidance on this note. The other three issues have not been addressed, and, in fact, the government has exacerbated the Freddie and Fannie problem by putting these Government Sponsored Entities into a conservatorship by the Federal Housing Finance Agency. They are now 100% government owned. Mortgage Backed Securities have not changed and are still a bundle of mortgages with no individual transparency and still rated by agencies to discover the problem associated with failing mortgages inside MMBs. What Dodd-Frank does to improve our banking situation is unclear as a small collective of banks are designated Too Big To Fail (what Congress considered the central problem but which is not) and have special privileges smaller banks do not enjoy. There are 2000 pages of new rules for banks and a Consumer Protection Bureau, but reading through a summary of reforms from the Senate Banking Committee doesn't provide a sense of comfort. Just one note should call attention to the many in the publication that actually do the opposite.

'**Independent Rule Writing:** Able to autonomously write rules for consumer protections governing all financial institutions – banks and non-banks – offering consumer financial services or products. ' (Dodd-Frank, 2010)

The unwritten warning is that a group of lawyers will be writing regulations that do not have the oversight of Congress. For the Left, this is considered good governance: special arrangements for big banks that can give big money to rent-seekers, regulation that does not fix the original issues that caused the meltdown and a bunch of unelected lawyers writing regulatory code?

Government command and control is essential to assure a cohesive national structure, but how much does over-micro-management cost Americans each year. The costs are not easy to measure, but outside of government Gartner Group has measured the cost of ineffective management via micro-management.

According to the book *12: The Elements of Great Managing* (Gallup Press, 2006), some benefit for process improvement (or adherence) may result from micro-management, but the biggest problem from someone looking over a worker's shoulder is lost trust. The result of lost trust is disengagement. Gallup research cited in the book finds that highly engaged teams average 18% higher productivity and 12% greater profitability than the least engaged teams. There should be little wonder that the end result of an increasingly micro-managed social environment whether in business or in our society at large trends more to the world of Winston Smith in Orwell's life in 1984 than what we would hope the typical Americans' life should be like.

What is nearly impossible to accurately present is not that micro-management is bad organizational theory for business or government personnel, but how much of the 18% higher productivity is sapped from our citizens by poorly conceived social policy, and centralized and micro-managed governance.

Deficiency Three: Government as Tax on Productivity/Innovation

If, as most economists believe that government is a tax on the productivity of a nation, then it should be our elected officials prime responsibility to minimize the cost of government to assure both domestic and international competitiveness. As Leftist governments tend to create solutions that government power and micro-manage some facet of our nation, as government grows, the burden of government increases. As the tax increases, our competitiveness is reduced, as is our economic freedom, private investment, productivity and even innovation, the ultimate driver of national economic success.

Robert J Gordon recently wrote in the Wall Street that between 1891 and 2007 the average increase in our annual output per person measured 2%. (Gordon, 2012) Two percent per year is a very big number. Gordon believes that only 1% productivity per annum is possible this century. He believes that innovation is not likely to add to the productivity gains as it has over the last two centuries. Although it is unlikely that his pessimism about the abatement of scientific discovery will actually occur, what is correct is that innovation is the result of capitalism (economic liberty) and rule of law via political liberty. As America moves away from liberalism – smaller government and more personal liberty - international competitors will begin attracting more and more innovators and technological entrepreneurs sapping America's productivity and economic activity of its life blood. A growing and more onerous government will increase the barriers to success for entrepreneurs who bring innovation and higher productivity. As government grows, innovation is diminished.

Joyce Appelby in The Relentless Revolution promotes capitalism (liberal economics) as the foundation for innovation.

'During the eighteenth century it became apparent for the first time that innovation was the secret, if uncertain, spring behind capitalism. I say "uncertain" because there is no way to compel innovation. (Appelby, 2010)

Reducing the positive effects of liberal economics abates innovation, which reduces productivity, which leaves America much where it is today, with low growth. Add then, the likelihood that the size of government will continue to increase the burden to business and individual, creating a perpetual glide path to slower and slower growth.

In 1891, the size of government (the tax on productivity) as a percentage of GDP was under 3%. Government's cost grew to 15% after WWII and then with the Carter Administration government spending hit 20% of GDP. By 1999-2000 Clinton managed to get spending down to 18.1% producing strong growth and a budget surplus. Under Obama spending has been at 24%, one-third higher than Clinton producing an economy stuck at 2% growth. Flash forward to 2030-2040, without reform of entitlements; spending will increase to 40% of GDP. If the economy were fairly healthy with government spending at 18.1% of GDP spending, and waning at 24% spending, imagine the economic response to a micro-managing government with spending at 40% of GDP. Also imagine poor Winston Smith's Economy that was fully managed by the government (picture the Soviet Union or Red China under Mao,) and know that social, cultural and economic growth was stuck at non-existent.

Winston Smith's homeland, Oceania, consumed 100% of its citizen's productivity. This heavy tax assured that Smith was the perfectly disengaged citizen, micro-managed into insignificance. No amount of good will, general will or good intentions can mask the effects of a giant bureaucracy looking over your shoulder. Trust is diminished, workers and voters disengage, productivity contracts and as government costs rise, our freedoms and capabilities are equally diminished.

Deficiency Four: Constitutional Monopolies

Government is a monopoly, as it has no competition. Once any government is formed, whether Kingdom, Republic or Tyranny, it is a high-energy dispenser of private and semi-private monopolies. Feudal Kings spewed vast numbers of monopolistic spiffs to their gentry in the form of land ownership or rights to bridges, roads and their tolls. Tyrannies take ownership of what they wish and the profits with them. Republics tend to rule with a lighter hand with less extensive reach, but America's history is filled with the likes of AT&T, local utilities, federal unions, and giant social monopolies.

What we seldom consider is that all of our government's constitutional responsibilities such as courts, law enforcement and the patent office were created as permanent monopolies. The military has no competition and wisely should not, and so is a monopoly. The Treasury prints money without competition. Prisons are not a competitive market though a private business may compete for a small local monopoly. Government is a monopoly, so defining the default foundation of government should help manage the government's girth.

Was the objective of a limited federal government to protect us against the inefficiencies of monopolies – to keep the government from expanding its footprint by creating monopolies for new roles? Not really. Though the answer may be yes, I am sure the worries of the Foundation Fathers were not so much about monopolies than about a deeper problem: too much centralized power. Those power and monopoly are not synonymous, monopolies could be the fuel to increase power.

Almost every new social responsibility the federal government has created over the last eight decades has been constructed as a monopoly: schools, Social Security, Medicare, Obamacare, the War on Poverty Programs, the Great Society programs, NASA and the Federal Highway system. Our elected officials seem to uniformly believe that social monopolies are the best structure to deploy government

44

services and social policy. The question whether a monopoly is the best solution for policy executive is debated but seldom with serious alternatives. A Liberal might ask, and certainly did during the Debates about Social Security and Obamacare, whether the government should expand outside its constitutional footprint, and if so if a government monopoly will actually deliver solutions of high value and low cost.

In 1954, Arnold Harberger wrote a pivotal and controversial paper, Monopoly and Resource Allocation, that stated that the actual misallocation of resources across industries due to monopolies or tariffs were actually quite small, as low as a fraction of a percent of GDP. "We come to the conclusion that monopoly misallocations entail a welfare loss of no more than a thirteenth of a per cent of the national income. Or, in present values, no more than about $1.40 per capita," he wrote. "I must confess that I was amazed at this result. . . . Monopoly does not seem to affect aggregate welfare very seriously through its effect on resource allocation" (Arnold Harberger, 2009) The paper was pivotal in that it animated much of the thinking about monopolies for decades, controversial in that it turned upside down the notion that monopolies were very inefficient allocators of resources.

In reality, though monopolies do not affect our general welfare in the aggregate, in specific industries their effect is quite notable.

James A. Schmtiz, in a recent paper for the Federal Reserve Bank of Minnesota, had a different analysis of monopolies and detailed resource allocations, not across industries but within industries with a much different result. Schmitz writes, 'From these histories a common theme (or theory) emerges as to why monopoly is costly. When a monopoly is created, "rents" are created. Conflict emerges among shareholders, managers, and employees of the monopoly as they negotiate how to divide these rents. Mechanisms are set up to split the rents. These mechanisms are often means to reduce competition among members of the monopoly. Although the mechanisms divide rents, they also destroy them (by leading to low productivity and misallocation).' (Schmitz, 2012)

Schmitz offers two important notions to any discussion of monopolies. First, that his definition is much broader and includes more than just private firms that control the production of a single industry. His definition also includes cartels and unions. Government monopolies are interestingly left out and a topic that will be discussed in this book. Second, he notes that as monopolies were destroyed in any particular industry that '(d)oubling of productivities in a few years was common. The value of the wasted inputs was as much as 20 percent to 30 percent of industry value added.'

Though few monopolies have been dismantled in the fast several decades, one does shed light as a common experience for us all, American Telephone and Telegraph. AT&T's breakup in 1884 was heralded by many and yet produced an immediate flurry of angst and anger by many consumers. This titanic monopoly, whose tariffs for local service and long distance was loved, was a necessary and expensive evil for much of the business world.

AT&T was a well-loved company. There was a single number to call. What could be simpler? Service was by any stretch of the imagination very good, and everyone had dial tone. On the downside, innovation in the telecom industry flagged and the expense for interstate services was high. Why, then, break up this well-loved monopoly. Bad economics and the exercise of political power.

AT&T's pricing structure had become a welfare state for residential services. An Ohio Bell official said early in 1983, "We're collecting, on the average, about $12 a month for basic local service from each residence customer. The gap between this $12 price and the $25 cost is currently recovered from other services priced considerably higher than their costs." (Barger, 1984) The other services were long distance tariffs and long-haul data services. For those old enough to remember, many long distances calls were over a $1 a minute. A point-to-point data line between New York and LA cost thousands of dollars.   Data services and long distance were highly profitable, enough so to cover the losses in local services.

Few privately held businesses would concede profitability in one division of a company with hopes of making up losses with the profits of another. Long Distance profits made up for losses in the residential services market, and as time proceeded so too did the glaring anomaly of misallocated resources. Ludwig von Mises shed light on the problem of a publically-regulated, private enterprise in his 1944 book *Bureaucracy*.

"But if a public enterprise is to be operated without regard to profits, the behavior of the public no longer provides a criterion of its usefulness. If the government or the municipal authorities are resolved to go on notwithstanding the fact that the operation costs are not made up by the payments received from the customers, where may a criterion be found of the usefulness of the services rendered? How can we find out whether the deficit is not too big with regard to these services? And how discover whether the deficit could not be reduced without impairing the value of the services?" (Mises, 1944)

More from Mises: "A private business is doomed if its operation brings losses only and no way can be found to remedy this situation. Its unprofitability is the proof of the fact that the consumers disallow it. There is, with private enterprise, no means of defying this verdict of the public and of keeping on. The manager of a plant involving a loss may explain and excuse the failure. But such apologies are of no avail; they cannot prevent the final abandonment of the unsuccessful project."

"It is different with a public enterprise. Here the appearance of a deficit is not considered a proof of failure. The manager is not responsible for it. It is the aim of his boss, the government, to sell at such a low price that a loss becomes unavoidable."

The voters in Ohio and in every state loved their subsidized phone service from this publically mandated monopoly.   The business people, though, who were the main voting block of users of long distance and data services, however, did not. There should be no doubt who ultimately had more clout as the misallocation of resources became evident. Large, interstate businesses were paying hundreds of millions of dollars in long distance and data communication services to assure that Joe in Toledo paid only $12 dollars for his phone per month. So in 1984, Judge Harold Green presided over the largest breakup of a monopoly in history.

The annoyance that followed that followed divestiture came from the challenge of having both a local provider of services (Baby Bells) and a long distance and data line provider between states. As important new competitors flowed into the market creating confusion for some consumers who enjoyed the one-size-fits-all solution of the former regime, new, less expensive solutions became available as well. The initial transition, though relatively smooth, brought competitive churn to an otherwise somnolent marketplace. As Schmitz suggested, after divestiture of the monopoly, great productivity enhancements filled the market. Long distance rates fell sharply. The cost of transmitting data fell precipitously, first from telecom competition, then from the Internet. New technology flooded the market in the form of cell phones and IP telephony. Ultimately the cost of long distance fell to zero. A land-line telephone via IP providers now costs about $20 a year! And 7MB data transmission for consumers is about $1.50 a day versus a T-1 (1.544Mbps) circa 1980 that could cost thousands of dollars. Picture phone services in the '70s started at $168 per month for data transmission costs plus the cost of the phone which rented for the same amount. Today, a phone with a data plan costs around $80 per month (family plans reduce the cost further) and the services are significantly better; phone, contacts, pictures, music, movies, internet service, and the picture phone. And it's mobile. Having all these services on a picture phone would have cost thousands and thousands of dollars pre-divestiture.

Our government wisely dismantled AT&T. Governments throughout history have created monopolies as a routine part of daily conduct. The East India Trading Company along with many others like it were conferred their right to do business as the sole agent in specified geographies throughout the world during the Renaissance. Naturally, the English Monarchy got a piece of the action for conferring such a special business opportunity. In France, tolls for roads and bridges were collected by barons who then paid tribute to the King. America began with small corporations extending investments to explorers, via a designated stock-funded monopoly allowed by the King. The first of these private, but government sponsored monopolies, the exploration of Virginia, turned out badly initially as the expectation of gold and silver never materialized. Later, when tobacco was discovered and new breeding techniques created profitable blends, the monopolistic investment created much wealth.

Modern government, *enlightened* government by Progressive standards, created a new type of monopoly in the twentieth century, the social monopoly. This new federal invention is one that little and perhaps no research regarding their effectiveness has been done. When Googling *Social Monopoly Efficiency* or *Social Monopoly* Google presents numerous results of the Social Costs of Monopolies but nothing about the efficiency or effectiveness of a Social Monopoly. So what is a social monopoly? As we pay nearly $2 trillion is taxes for these government entities, we should all know, but these entities are not something we think of as monopolies. They are Federal Programs to *help* us. In reality, though, Social Security, Medicare, Schools, Medicare, Great Society and War on Poverty programs are monopolies run by the government and paid for by taxes.

Schmitz could easily have had a discussion of the federal pension monopoly, Social Security. Today, the unfunded liability is just over $7 trillion. An easy argument can be made that taxing the working population to pay benefits to the non-working seniors is not very efficient. Most important, as not one dollar of these taxes are saved or invested exacerbates that inefficiency significantly. The most celebrated case of moving a public pension system to a personal private solution comes from Chili where there conversion from public social security to a personal savings system has not only produced higher pension payouts but where their economy has had growth easily double the US's and lower unemployment rates.

Deficiency Five: Government Social Monopolies

'The clear and direct tendency of the poor laws, is in direct opposition to these obvious principles: it is not, as the legislature benevolently intended, to amend the condition of the poor, but to deteriorate the condition of both poor and rich; instead of making the poor rich, they are calculated to make the rich poor; and whilst the present laws are in force, it is quite in the natural order of things that the fund for the maintenance of the poor should progressively increase, till it has absorbed all the neat revenue of the country, or at least so much of it as the state shall leave to us, after satisfying its own never failing demands for the public expenditure.' (Richardo, 2011, Locations 940-945)

In this comment from David Ricardo published over two hundred years ago, great advice is given. Is the job of government to make the rich poor, or the poor richer? This seems to have been the case of the last eight decades. Government policy has and is promoting a set of notions that seem to assure both the rich and the poor are no better off after having the benefit of government advice and expenditure.

The notion that only the government can effectively run social policy and services programs is based on no empirical data. Further, executing social policy via a set of mandated government monopolies is not supported by organizational or economic data regarding their potential for efficiency or effectiveness. A fairly good case could be made that social policy implemented via a monopoly is likely the poorest option available to government. Yet Leftist political will seeking political power via Progressive politics launched in America during the early part of the twentieth century is responsible for these super-sized and highly underfunded monopolies. Political will comes in the form of the snobbery of the Left that assumes a central role for top-down social engineering. Political power arrives with expensive monopolies that require the guiding hand of the political elite. Neither efficiency nor effectiveness is the objective. Consumption of political power in the name of *good intentions* is. The road to hell, as we all know is paved by these good intentions.

Social Security, America's national, Progressive social insurance monopoly did not easily pass muster of Congress, FDR or the Supreme Court. FDR did not want the program paid for out of general revenues but with a separate tax that would pay for the program. The Republicans in Congress did not want to participate in this new experiment and were labeled Conservatives for their efforts. After Congressional passage that included a fixed tax rate of 1% on income to cover the costs of Social Security, FDR ultimately challenged the Supreme Court justices with Court packing to assure the final negotiated package from Congress would be enacted with its blessing as he knew this new government mission into uncharted social, economic and political territory would be legally challenged. FDR's muscle flexing to sway the Supreme Court managed to assure the Progressive will of the moment.

In 1936, the Supreme Court finally reviewed lower court decisions regarding the federal government's ability to collect taxes and the use of funding for underwriting our nation's 'general welfare.' During our nation's early years a discussion between the Federalists and Anti-Federalist a discussion of such taxation had already occurred between Madison and Hamilton. Over the course of the next century and a half Hamilton's view that taxes could be spent for any need for the nation's general welfare won the day. Per Justice Cardozo, who wrote the decision for Helvering vs. Davis, he comments:

> "Congress may spend money in aid of the "general welfare". Constitution, Art. I, section 8; *United States v. Butler*, 297 U. S. *1, 65*; *Steward Machine Co. v. Davis, supra.* There have been great statesmen in our history who have stood for other views. We will not resurrect

the contest. It is now settled by decision. *United States v. Butler, supra* The conception of the spending power advocated by Hamilton and strongly reinforced by Story has prevailed over that of Madison, which has not been lacking in adherents. Yet difficulties are left when the power is conceded. The line must still be drawn between one welfare and another, between particular and general. Where this shall be placed cannot be known through a formula in advance of the event. There is a middle ground or certainly a penumbra in which discretion is at large. The discretion, however, is not confided to the courts. The discretion belongs to Congress, unless the choice is clearly wrong, a display of arbitrary power is not an exercise of judgment."

A Republican resolution was not at hand, and though the Supreme Court Justice commented about where 'the line must still be drawn between one welfare state and another, between particular and general,' he left where that line to be defined to the power vested in Congress. Just Right for moment allow the erection of America's first social Monopoly. Basically, since this decision, there is no throttle on government spending or government ventures into social monopolies but a Congress whose appetite to spend to *improve* the general welfare has had few bounds. The decision was a complete flailing of any notion of Liberalism and limited government. The government could *damned well* do what it pleased and spend what it pleased unless the citizens sent their Congressmen to the side of the road. This argument would again be used by Justice Roberts in 2012 when he argued that Obamacare's mandates to purchase insurance was a tax, and that, additionally, it was not the responsibility of the courts to fix poorly written laws.

"Members of this Court are vested with the authority to interpret the law; we possess neither the expertise nor the prerogative to make policy judgments. Those decisions are entrusted to our Nation's elected leaders, who can be thrown out of office if the people disagree with them. It is not our job to protect the people from the consequences of their political choices." (Roberts, 2012)

What, then, does the definition of an effective government mean when the two branches that should restrain each other from excesses of power have been provided unbridled power by a Supreme Court that is queasy about any limits for the other branches? In this condition our government has moved far to the Left using General Welfare to mimic Rousseau's 'general will' and 'forcing citizens to be free' while dispensing an endless supply of government chits that are driving us quickly to bankruptcy.

What becomes evident over the course of these decades since FDR is that Congress without any curbs on spending expands government in general, and social monopolies in specific, faster that the growth or the economy and the population. Translated into economic terms: the cost of government monopolies is growing faster than the government's ability to collect taxes for them. During the Obama and Bush administrations alone Food Stamp qualifications were reduced allowing the number of recipients to rise from just under 25 million in 2000 to nearly 47 million in 2012. Medicaid changes (additional benefits) are listed nicely in a Kaiser Foundation document with three pages of bulleted items of qualification updates and program entitlement expansions. Social Security that started as an insurance program to pool risk for aged who had retired at 65 which was three years over life expectancy was expanded national pension system for families by 1950, and expanded to include disabilities and other programs in the same decade. And our schools have gone from local school house in the early 20th century to a three-tiered government monopoly whose restrictive government oversight has most recently added another set of complicated strictures in Bush's No Child Left Behind.

If government monopolies were effective tools for creating a Great Society then the following social metrics could not have occurred over the last several decades.

- Marriage rate is down 36%. The corresponding variable, illegitimacy is up 36%.
- Educational Attainment: Flat for the last 35 years despite increased spending (in real dollars) of 200%.
- Poverty Rate: Substantially unchanged since the inception of the War on Poverty despite trillions in spending since 1967
- Savings Rate: Down 900% since 1950
- Unfunded Federal Retirement Benefits: $47 Trillion per Heritage Foundation.
- Average GDP Growth: A declining record for GDP growth (with some small ups and downs) over the last 60 years.
- National Debt: Growth from around 30% of GDP 1980 to over 100% today.

The question the Supreme Court could in fact determine 'are these monopolistic outcomes actually promoting the general welfare of America and Americans?' The answer is an easy, 'No!' As important shouldn't social policy produce social programs whose outcomes produce more American's capable of success. A great social program would, over time, reduce dependence on government. Just the opposite is occurring, social welfare rolls are increasing.

Deficiency Six: Costs of Social Monopoly Failure

Although I am not an economist, I do have a degree in Mathematics and so am keenly interested in the numbers, good or bad. Two financial outputs are manifest: 1) the current and future unfunded costs for unbridled social welfare monopolies, especially Social Security and Medicare are well calculated and astronomical - $44 trillion, and 2) our current Great Society social policy should produce a fewer and fewer recipients as social programs engage recipients in a way that launches them on a path to success and away from government support, but do not.

The problem is then four-fold, 1) current social policy is erected on an organizational platform (micro-managed monopoly) that is inefficient, ineffective and very costly, 2) the general social policy of handing checks to clients is not working to produce fewer clients but more, 3) the cost of these programs erodes economic growth reducing opportunity, especially among the poor and uneducated, and 4) our national social policy is based on the intellectually notion historically understood to be ineffective: give a man a fish...?

Problems two through four are deeply engraved in the poor economic performance of America's social monopolies. Understanding the costs of our broken social policy and poor implementation of that policy will help frame the scope of America's economic decline that results from these policies.

Lost Opportunity Cost of National Debt: -1.4% of GDP

As America is currently borrowing to support a bevy of social programs, let's start with debt.

Over the last few decades American's have been told that debt and deficits are not important. And not just the Left has suggested there is no cost to accruing debt. Even Republicans chimed in.   During the Reagan Administration, Dick Cheney said to Paul O'Neal, the Secretary of the Treasury, 'You know, Paul, Reagan proved that deficits don't matter. We won the mid-term elections, this is our due.' (Cheney, 2013) Democrats and Keynesians would say that borrowing money from ourselves (most of America's debt is financed by the purchase of Treasury Bonds by Americans) has no economic penalty, but there is much to prove this notion invalid. And the fact of the matter. Low debt may be less harmful even hard to measure, but large and growing debt has been proved economic painful.

Anyone can attest to how credit card debt in their personal budgets is not much of a problem when these debts are low. When the credit card holder hopes to make credit card payment by acquiring new credit cards, the house of credits cards begins to fall. To acquire a mortgage on a new home, banks have generally required that income to debt ratio be in the high thirties. Dodd Frank now has this rate at 43%. (CRA International, 2006) (Pozen, 2013) The European Union mandates a 40% range for candidates to apply for membership. The acceptability of debt at the 40% range seems to be a norm in our common business practices. More important, any notion that high debt produces economic growth is intellectually empty. A Google search for 'high debt, high growth' netted a single response. One! The Search did produce a vast array of 'high debt, low growth' links. One paper, *Public Debt and Growth* summarized the harsh realities of high debt by reviewing the economies of both emerging economies and mature economies. From the summary:

> 'The empirical results suggest an inverse relationship
> between initial debt and subsequent growth,
> controlling for other determinants of growth: on
> average, a 10 percentage point increase in the initial
> debt-to-GDP ratio is associated with a slowdown in
> annual real per capita GDP growth of around 0.2
> percentage points per year, with the impact being

somewhat smaller in advanced economies.'
(Manmohan S. Kumar, 2010)

The net of the drag on the economy due to high debt, which was under 30% during the Carter administration and it over 100% today, is 7 times .2% or 1.4%. Consider that an economy running at 3.4% instead of 2% would mean a great deal of employment opportunities for those that have no options. On the current borrowing binge, our indebtedness will reach $25 trillion this decade. Michael Peterson of the Peter G. Peterson Foundation, a think tank dedicated to public awareness of America's fiscal challenges said, 'The primary goal of any sustainable fiscal policy is to stabilize the debt as a share of the economy and put it on a downward path, and yet our nation is still heading toward debt levels of 200 per cent of GDP and beyond.' (Needham, 2013) At 200% of GDP, the negative drag on GDP would be 3.4%.

Even President Obama's Council of Economic Advisors buttressed the notion of debt creating a burden on growth.

> 'We therefore use the relatively conservative rule of thumb that a 1 percent increase in GDP corresponds to an increase in employment of approximately 1 million jobs, or about three-quarters of a percent.' (President, 2009)

In 2010 Harvard's Carmen Reinhart and Kenneth Rogoff added to the debt harm theory with research that covered 200 years. Their conclusions about major industrial economies boiled down to:

> 'Our main findings are: First, the relationship between government debt and real GDP growth is weak for debt/GDP ratios below a threshold of 90 percent of GDP. Above 90 percent, median growth rates fall by one percent, and average growth falls considerably more. We find that the threshold for public debt is

similar in advanced and emerging economies.' (Carmen Reinhard, 2010)

To both confuse and yet refine the debt/growth debate, Thomas Herndon of University of Massachusetts in Amhurst published research that challenged Reinhart and Rogoff's findings. Errors in the statistics were discovered that mitigated their findings, reducing the effects of increasing indebtedness. Paul Krugman announced that the new findings validated his notion that he, like Maynard Keynes, believed that governments can create internal debt with impunity. This is likely an overstatement as noted by the Weekly Standard:

> 'In fact, though, they don't. HAP's recalculations of RR's data eliminate the dramatic drop-off in growth rates at the 90 percent ratio. But they also show an unmistakable drift toward slower growth as the debt ratio rises. Countries with up to 30 percent debt-to-GDP ratio, according to HAP's paper, average 4.2 percent growth; growth falls to 3.1 percent at a 60 percent ratio. Growth increases to 3.2 percent as the ratio reaches 90 percent. After 90 percent, growth averages 2.2 percent.
>
> In other words, by the time a debt ratio rises above 90 percent of GDP, growth will be cut roughly in half—according to HAP's own calculations. High debt-GDP ratios, once they take hold in a country, tend to last for 15 years or more. An annual loss of 2 percentage points in growth over such a sustained period really starts to add up:' (Ferguson, 2013)

Borrowing (and spending) our way to prosperity is not a workable   solution.

Education Monopoly Ineffectiveness: -9.0% of GDP

What is evident about America's current state of education is that about 25% of our citizens receive a poor to bad education. Another quarter of American children receive less than adequate education. Without a quality education, the lowest economic quartile of our citizens, people that should be participants in American Success, don't have an on ramp to the American Dream. Economic impacts for less than stellar education are all over the board, but the costs are always high.

From a McKinsey and Co. investigation, Robert Tomsho of the Wall Street found these statistics:

> "Closing the educational-achievement gap between the U.S. and higher-performing nations such as Finland and South Korea could boost U.S. gross domestic product by as much as $2.3 trillion, or about 16%, according to a new study by McKinsey & Co., the international consulting concern.
>
> The report, which used a formula McKinsey helped develop to link educational achievement to economic output, also estimated closing the gap in the U.S. between white students and their black and Latino peers could increase annual GDP by as much as an additional $525 billion, or about 4%." (Tomsho, 2009)

A 16% increase in GDP is generous, even fabulous, and hopefully not wishful speculation, so I will be a bit more conservative. Here's the math:

As the bottom 50% of income earners totaled just under $1 trillion in income for 2010 according to IRS research data, and GDP totaled $15 trillion, increasing productivity and capability in the bottom 50% of earners by $2.3 (16% of GDDP) trillion or $230% seems a bit of a challenge. That is if they only produced $1 trillion in income, $2.3 trillion is a gigantic economic leap.

Per the Census Bureau 9.1% of 16-24 year olds have no high school diploma. Though the dropout rate has declined from the mid-teens in the '70s to the current 9.1% today, using a 10% average is a kind number to use. Also, per the Census Bureau there are just over 200 million Americans of working age. The bottom 50% would be the bottom 100 million. If on average 10 percent of these workers do not have the benefit of a high school education (assume all 20 million non-grads are in the bottom half of tax payers) and per the Georgetown publication 'The College Payoff' the average dropout earns $973,000 versus $1.3 million for a high school graduate, or $327,000 over a lifetime (about $8,000 a year in a straight line division, then the gross incremental income during the current year for a better education for dropout would be only $160 billion (not close to the $2.3 trillion for McKinnsey.)

Assuming the other 80 million people in the 100 million low earners obtained a high quality of education and obtained another $160 billion in value, a better education for low income Americans would have only a 2% ($329B) incremental value to our GDP. There are other advantages. A better education generally means a higher likelihood to marry, a benefit that reduces the need for government assistance. The better one's education, the better one's health and general quality of life. In fact, for persons that get an education, getting a job (or two) and getting married, 98% of these cohorts have no need for government programs. This would reduce the cost of the Federal social welfare monopolies, by around 95%, or just under $500 billion, or another 3% of GDP.

So to be fair-minded in determining a number that we could use: rather than McKinsey's 16%, a kinder, gentler notion of a low of 2% and high of 6% is a better barometer.

Government Health Monopolies: Cost to GDP: 2.6% and Rising

There are more than a few socio-economic variables that increase costs for healthcare for Americans. A lack of an education leads to increased morality rates. An enduring marriage has positive health benefits. The complexity of regulation is a heavy expense we all pay as well. The focus of this section will be with cost shifting – the amount of money privately insured American's pay for government subsidized healthcare.

Medicaid, Medicare, Obamacare have much the same problem that AT&T had. AT&T fixed below cost prices for local telephone service to assure residential clients a low price and made up losses by charging artificially high prices for long distance calls. American healthcare is not immune to this kind of government pricing dysfunction. Since the advent of Medicare and Medicaid Congress has fixed prices for services paid by government that were either near or below cost for providers. The distortion of this price fixing shows up as increased costs for privately paid health care.

Price-fixing is one of two major tools the government only for cost reduction. The second, eliminating services is seldom used. More often the government is in the business of expanding services as a method of obtaining votes. Reducing costs via innovation and continuous process improvement because neither government nor monopolies are possessed with skills or desire to do either. As there are no competitive forces, either business-centric or political no competitive forces exist to engage these economic forces. Thus the only tool available is price-fixing. The 'fee for service' solution, Congress' legislative mechanism for fixing prices, causes severe problems for providers in two ways: 1) not enough dollars in the exchange for the service to render it a valuable solution for the customer or the provider, and 2) fewer and fewer doctors willing to provide these services for government healthcare as the lower costs affected their ability to provide a living for themselves. By law, hospitals are forced to participate in Medicare or Medicaid because they are mandated to take patients in emergency rooms regardless of their ability to pay or their type of payment.

To mitigate this 'too few dollars for a service' problem, providers do what AT&T did, they make up for losses in government provided services by increasing prices for the privately insured. Government intrusion has led to 'cost shifting' from public to private, costing the typical private insurance customer between 3% to 5% of their premium, and, in the coming decades with significant additions to the public health insurance market via boomers for Medicare and expansions in Medicaid and Obamacare, up to 15% of their premium. Today, the average Family of four insures for $15,000 per year (according to the Kaiser Family Foundation) including up to $2,250 in cost shifting.

This is one of two costs paid by the private insurer. The second cost is taxes paid for government health programs for which no services are rendered to the private insurer.

One hundred and ninety-five million persons with private insurance also pay taxes for Medicare and Medicaid largely for a group of government healthcare clients that do not pay taxes or only a tiny fraction of their benefit. Estimating for the average tax payer who earns the median income of $50,000 @ 1.45% tax for Medicare is $725. Add on another $725 (Federal Medicare and Medicaid outlays are currently about the same) in federal taxes that goes to Medicaid and the grand total a working citizen pays over and above insurance only for he and his family comes to $3,700. Add it all up - and 115 million households (according to the Census Bureau) pay $420 billion in taxes and additional insurance costs. That is a chunk of change.

Obamacare will attempt to reduce costs by forcing young, healthy citizens to buy expensive insurance or face a fine. Though few in the Obama administration will state that the objective of this mandate is to provide money to Medicare and Medicaid to reduce the effect of rapid rises in costs for these programs, this is the precise intent. Reverse cost shifting if you will. The new, young enrollees to Obamacare with be like the former long distance customers for AT&T,

the premium payers for service. As of September 2013, 13 states that had set up insurance exchanges, the average increase in premiums was 24% according to Forbes Magazine. (Roy, Interactive Map: In 13 States Plus DC Obamacare Will Increase Health Premiums by 24% on Average, 2013) Even with this reverse cost-shifting employed the $37 trillion unfunded liability for Medicare will be only slightly diminished.

For the typical family, then, total personal productivity is reduced $3700 or an average 7.4% of the median household income of $50,000. Productive citizens are paying for the inefficiency of government monopolies. In GDP terms the above $420 billion cost shifting is 2.6%, another large hit to America's productivity.

For many on the Left this 2.6% hit to productivity is a small price to pay to assure that the poor and elderly have health insurance. This idea is based on a near religious belief that only a government monopoly can deliver healthcare for these groups, which is not the case. Most certainly as the quality of government healthcare continues to diminish, private and or personal financing solutions will provide much less expensive and higher quality outcomes. But more on this in Efficiencies of Liberal Governance.

Social Security and Medicare: Tax versus Save

Every American pays 6.2% of income in taxes to support America's forty million Social Security recipients and 1.45% for Medicare. The businesses we work for are taxed the same amount. In 2012, Americans we paid $795 billion in taxes. Retired beneficiaries paid an additional $111 billion in taxes on benefits and additional insurance premiums for Medicare Part D. The government paid out $1.36 trillion to recipients. The $453 billion deficit was paid out of the general fund. The national press and government often promulgate the idea that the difference between tax revenue for these programs and paid benefits are made up with a Trust Fund of surplus tax revenues of these programs from the last few decades. To be absolutely clear: there is no trust fund. The surpluses from past years were spent during the same year the surplus was created. All the money, over $2 trillion has been spent. The system is already bankrupt.

Were this 6.4% tax of Social Security and 1.45% tax for Medicare either saved or invested at even a nominal rate of return, the net change in our economic well-being is astronomical. Cumulatively, the effects are vast, erasing an unfunded mandate of $44 trillion over the next 75 years and producing a vast array of personal nest eggs over the next 40 years' worth about $100 trillion. This is a net change in private investment with respect to cumulative GDP of over 11%. This net change of government borrowing to personal and corporate investment would heighten America position as the financial capital of the world, keeping China and the European Union at bay, and producing tens of millions of jobs. The greatest effect though is that hundreds of millions of Americans would have their own personal nest eggs available for production of more wealth and a quiet, safe, delightful retirement. That we have a tax-based versus savings based retirement system is a mind boggling mental disability of great proportion. What rational, disinterested, Leftist could possibly purpose a solution that would cripple individuals and do grave harm to the economy as the current tax-based solution? Hopefully, no rational human would advocate the mindless continuation an solution that might have been a good fit 100 years ago, but is now creating program deficits of nearly $500 billion which will soon rise to $1 trillion, then $2 trillion then more.

The current funding mechanism for retirement is financially unsustainable. Pegging benefits to some artificially set age is just the first problem.

Had the Social Security Administration pegged benefits to average life expectancy plus three years (in 1933 life expectancy was 65 years of age) instead of fixing the age of retirement at 65, there would likely be a surplus for Social Security and Medicare today. Today, the retirement age would be 79. Congress did not have a very clear vision of a future with life expectancy which will reach 100 years of age sometime this century. Fixing the age at 65 and adding more and more benefits, expanding the number of type of beneficiaries to the program has required that taxes be raised from 1% of income to 6.2%. Today, the Social Security Administration states that taxes for both Social Security and Medicare will need to rise to nearly 15% of income to pay beneficiaries through 2050.

So Congress created a monopoly built on poor financial reasoning that today has produced a solution whose end point is either more taxes or less benefits, and as our life expectancy increases perpetually, Congress will again and again have to come to the table with request after request to either raise taxes or reduce benefits.

Great harm is done to Americans, especially the poor who must pay Social Security taxes. Social Security and Medicare taxes are the highest taxes taken from their paychecks. The well off get a break, because the Social Security Tax is not paid on income of $105,000 a number which is adjusted up each year via the Consumer Price Index. The poor get the least benefit, because not only is their payout lower, the working class lives shorter lives.

It is a bit hard to imagine a set of programs that could be more ill-conceived financially – solutions that perpetually increase taxes without ever creating one dime of wealth. To make matters worse, these programs are on legislative auto glide. Congress does not vote on the increases in benefits each year, and for Medicare, an occasional vote is exercised to reduce fee for Medicare services. No one is at the wheel. Imagine running a financial services company like this. Most assuredly, its leaders would be indicted after only a few quarters of skirting their fiduciary responsibilities. In America, though leaders that act this irresponsibly get re-elected.

Citizen Disengagement: -??%

Micromanagement of social welfare via government monopoly has led to an increasingly obvious production of a permanent underclass and a diminishing voter class. The effects of social micro-management have been discussed above and are significant. What are lost in the numbers are the lives that are depreciated by government checks and chits that create learned dependence.

'The opposite of earned success is "learned helplessness," a term coined by Martin Seligman, the eminent psychologist at the University of Pennsylvania. It refers to what happens if rewards and punishments are not tied to merit: People simply give up and stop trying to succeed.' (Brooks, 2012)

The monetary value of learned helplessness is high. Continued political support for government social monopolies assure that large segments of our society have either no ability or severely hampered abilities to drive onto the on ramp of the American Dream. Without access to work, education and family all but guarantees the well-being of millions is weakened. Per Seligman: "We found that even when good things occurred that weren't earned, like nickels coming out of slot machines, it did not increase people's well-being."[1] As much as the Left complains about Capitalism and its focus on material wealth over personal growth, the Left has focused solely on material cash transfers that are like so many nickels coming from slots machines, not the personal growth that comes from work, family and a real liberal education (something completely missing in many of our inner city schools.) If the 'entitled' franchise at the bottom of America's economic ladder awakes one day and understands how they have been uniformly kept from the liberation of 'earned success,' the revolt will be ugly.

Voters have already revolted, but without much effect. Both parties continue to send 'rent seekers' to Congress who do much the same as their previous peers by continuing the status quo. Many other voters have simply given up and either do not register to vote of simply do not vote. The costly result here is that America is stuck in no man's land, unable to move to a smarter wiser style of governance and assuring the size and scope of government monopolies grow out of control.

---

[1] Ibid

Cost Summary: What Poor Social Engineering Costs America

The bad news for the Left is that the total negative effect of social monopolies is not calculated by simply adding the below percentages equaling 16.45%. Like much in economics, variables tend to affect one another. It is likely the social and financial cost of Leftist social policy is actually worse. The object of this economic exercise is to estimate a conservative number that should promote debate to discover better solutions. For Liberal's in America, the good newsis that is hard to imagine how any competing solution could produce worse numbers.

- Debt: - 1.2% of GDP and increasing
- Education: -5% GDP and flat
- Healthcare: -2.6% of GCP and increasing to 6% by mid-century
- Social Security and Medicare: -5% of GDP (estimated taxes as percent of GDP) - the loss of potential investment income over the next 40 years totals over $100 trillion
- Disengagement: Not easily measurable, but is visible in Marriage Rate, dropout rate, voter apathy

These numbers show a slow but assured disintegration of our economy, our society and our culture under the heavy hand of a strong central, Leftist government. The economics are easy to forecast. If we do not manage to solve our debt problem, we will either run over an economic cliff when other nations decide not to fund our excesses, or we find simply run into a long-term economic malaise that will make us a second-class power and at the mercy of countries who will willingly take our place at the helm of a new world order.

Deficiency Seven: Centralized Power

As the founding fathers discovered that too little central power did not produce a national civil society, the examples of too much power that resonated throughout the history that preceded them produced all too many including their own King, King George. As there were no suitable examples of the liberal government they wished, they produced something new, a federal government whose powers they limited to secure, perpetually, the liberties of the people.

Our Leftist governance over the last centuries, governance that increased federal power eight fold, has generated two unintended consequences to our prosperity and liberty: an unbalanced power relationship between federal government and state governments and their citizens. The increasing power of the federal government has produced steady reductions in the sovereignty of the states and liberties of the citizens. The appetite for power in Washington seems to have no end and political greed (rent-seeking) has led to political stasis and status quo thinking.

Power *is* an essential requirement for effective government. As government has monopolies for several constitutional responsibilities including defense of America against enemies, adjudication of law, regulation commerce, coining money, and creating treaties with foreign agents, the power to execute its responsibilities is complete 'even with death itself' as a penalty should the offense of law be great.

Absolute power to execute law should not be confused to the consumption, use and excessive execution of too much accumulated power in the central authority.

Craig Zucker is an inventor and entrepreneur. He is the stuff American's at their best are made of. He describes himself as a serial entrepreneur. Even better! Craig built a toy made for any executives' desk, Buckyballs's, a collection of rare earth magnets that can be aligned to make an plethora of shapes. Per a Wall Street Journal, he built his business first by word of mouth, then by acquiring better and better marketing and distribution. (Ahmari, 2013) Then every citizen's worst nightmare occurred. Well, maybe second worst nightmare. The letter he received wasn't from the IRS. It was from the Consumer Product Safety Commission. It was a letter saying that a 'corrective-action' which Zucker dutifully sent, but which was rejected. A total recall was demanded because the magnets could pose a risk children, though the product packaging was clearly label for 13+ per guidelines provided … yep, by the Federal government. The commission concomitantly sent out letters to Zucker's resellers who, wanting no beef with the feds, dropped his product. Mr. Zucker was put out of business because a government agency decided that Buckyballs have a 'low utility for consumers and 'are not necessary to consumers.' The government put Mr. Zucker out of business because they 'felt' the product provides no value. Really. Our government? The commission added insult to injury by filing a lawsuit against Mr. Zucker as the CEO claiming he should be held personally reasonable for the cost of the recall, about $57 million. And this for a product of low utility and unnecessary to their vastly adult customer base for which no claims of harm to children has been produced. A bit nuts, eh.

Perhaps a call from the IRS would have been more judicious. Do note, that calling the IRS for advice, should you get the automated attendant first, the caller will be alerted to the fact that no advice given is necessarily correct.

Closer to home, many of us have heard stories not unlike what a friend of our family went through. The Smiths are an Arizona family with three generations of men and women who are farmers. The grandfather was a former San Francisco Giant running back that moved back to Maricopa, Arizona to work the land. His son, Matt, spawned a different kind of farming business, growing grass – no, the real stuff, not the stuff you smoke. He and his wife Elena are the salt of the earth. Plain speaking, good humored, very hard working. During a transition where they would sell their business to their children, the Department of Transportation showed up to audit their fleet of trucks – ten trucks that mostly haul grass to customer sites.

The feds showed up, for ten trucks. Really. It should make all of us wonder how the feds have so much time on their hands to audit Matt. Regardless, the compliance regulations were so complicated they had to hire a consultant to unravel the mass of tangled red tape. But the worst part of the whole ordeal, beyond wasting of much money painting the DOT Registration Numbers on every truck, was the fact that the consultant had to explain far too much of the regulatory issues to the DOT official. That is, more perfectly, the regulation is so complicated that the government doesn't understand them either. Just like the IRS automated attendant warning that they may not have all the right answers, it appears DOT doesn't either.

Back in Washington this year, the IRS had singled out Tea Party organization to deprive them of tax exempt status for operation of their organizations. The NSA was found to vastly exceed its FISA orders in tapping into phone records around the world and in the United States. The president on more than one occasion end ran the Congress and order by fiat resident status for many illegals to provide access to American Colleges. This was a very nice thing to do but not the way business is conducted in a Democracy. The EPA issued orders on the regulation of carbon dioxide though there has been no enabling legislation for CO2 as a hazardous material. And these are only examples from this President's second term, many this year.

Yet these examples are just the tip of the iceberg as government is so big, so complicated, it's not only impossible for us and the businesses we work for to figure out how to comply to a vast reservoir of regulation, even the government and its vast membership of bureaucrats are just as confused as we are.

Although blaming individuals who consume and execute power like tyrants is easy and reasonable, we as citizens have to understand that most people don't go to Washington to bath in the delights of centralized power; almost no one takes up residence there to find ways to minimize the Federal footprint. Politicians and bureaucrats with the best of intentions are devoured by the culture of power. But power does have two faces, one Leftist with the specific intent to expand the power in the central government, and one Liberal that seeks to empower those entities for which it is responsible to lead – the people. The examples of the former are numerous. The examples of the latter are few and far between.

If power is money and money is without question one source of great power, then consolidation of power in the federal government has been on a century long upswing. The following chart is compiled from statistical information from usgovernmentspending.com.

Federal Power (Budget) Increases of Last Century

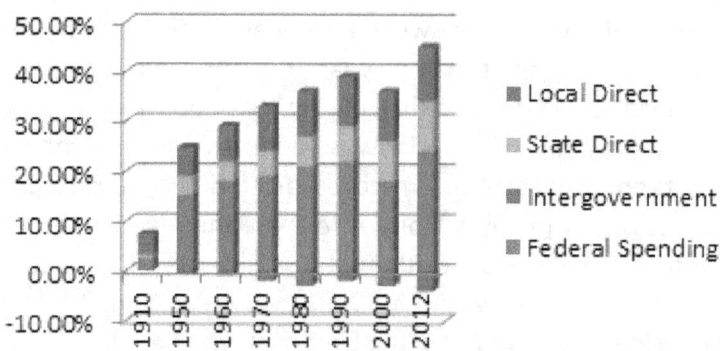

Figure 1: **Historical Federal, State and Local Spending as a Percent of GDP**

By 2050, Heritage Foundation estimates, should Congress commit to neither tax nor spending changes, federal spending will exceed 40% of GDP and revenues will likely hold steady at around 18% of GDP. As federal spending increases it is also likely that federal mandates to states will increase as well. The red bars are transfers of Federal dollars that must be matched by the states, i.e. federal mandates. The biggest of these programs is Medicaid. This expensive and low-quality solution for low-income health care is about to be trumped by additional expense to the state in the form of Obamacare, further saddling states with expense.

As the Judiciary has given nearly unlimited Constitutional power to Congress to tax and spend, the federal government has taken an increasing large share of the total political power. Expanding government monopolies that dispense dollars or benefits via chits for services assure a larger and larger voting public that seeks rents from the government for subsistence.

Federal Budget Estimates 2000 - 2050

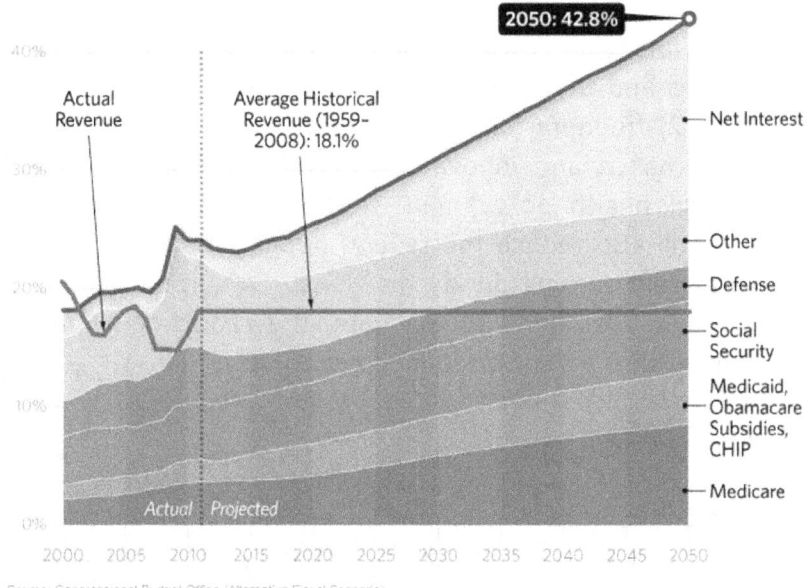

Without Reform Fed Spending Will Exceed 40% of GDP by 2050

The states have lost considerable power as federal mandates for spending have trended up from a small part of their budgets in 1970 where education budgets were generally half to two-thirds of most states budgets, to today where federal mandated state spending consumes nearly one-third of the budget and another third for dollars mandated by ballot initiatives leaving the primary responsibilities of the state (education, roads, law enforcement, etc.) to go begging for the other third. To put the numbers in context, presume a state has a $10 billion budget and $6.7 billion are federal mandates ballot initiatives that cannot be reduced when there is a budget downturn. If revenues shrink 10% or $1 billion, legislators must find that $1 billion in cuts from the one-third of their $3.3 billion budget they actually control. The remainder of the budget is untouchable.

In the 1980s, legislatures had much more responsibility over a larger percentage of the budget, 70% to 80% percent of the budget. Finding $1 billion of reductions in $7 billion or $8 billion is a far easier task.

Rebalancing the power structure provides three valuable assets for states and the people: 1) more efficient management of state budgets, 2) freedom for states to become incubators of new ideas for governance and innovators for best practices in social, educational and health policy, and 3) the resulting reduction in responsibility will also reduce the federal budget and therefore the powerbase for rent-seeking during elections. A corollary effect in those states that use liberal to innovate, the reduction in micro-management will also reduce *disengagement* of its citizens.

Political Greed

For business, growth is important enabling financial success. Shrinking income general means trouble for stock value. Businesses measure success via an income statement and balance sheet. Good results are captured in rising revenues and increasing profits, presented in audited financial statements and published to markets and the world. Rising profitability increases the number of employees and an expanding physical footprint. Our personal ledgers are much the same. When our incomes rise and additional discretionary income can be spent on the nicer things in life, we feel the quality of our material lives increase.

So like a business executive, most of our political leaders believe that growth in government is good. And like many business leaders, there is a certain greed that accompanies a focus on growth. Additional political power accrues when government grows. Government grows by both increasing funding in areas that are its inherent constitutional responsibilities such as the military, and also through the creation of new products like Social Security and Obamacare. Power is also accrued by dispensing credits for businesses which adds to their profits and fattens the war chests of politicians.

Because government has no profit motive, no focus on quality, and no governance directed at efficiency, political power is highly focused on budget growth. Government success in growing the budget assures an increasing stream of fundraising from a growing group of special interests producing greater and greater funding for political campaigns. As budgets grow more and more is at stake when dividing up the federal budget pie. Those budget dollars are protected and increased annually by political rent-seeking which fuels campaigns to assure that more budget dollars are accrued and spent, which in turn creates more power and rent seeking. This deadly double helix of power seeking growth is producing a black hole in Washington.

Politicians will say just about anything to assure spending increases. President Obama delivered this odd notice to Americans in late 2013, 'Now, this debt ceiling -- I just want to remind people in case you haven't been keeping up -- raising the debt ceiling, which has been done over a hundred times, does not increase our debt.' (Obama, Obama: 'Raising the Debt Ceiling...Does Not Increase Our Debt,' Though It Has 'Over 100 Times', 2013) Oddly, this is good lawyer-speak, because in fact the debt is not increased one penny when the limit is increased. But, like increasing the limit on our credit cards when we have maxed our cards out, we generally do not ask for the increase so we can spend less. Congress dutifully follows any debt limit increase, using it to fund more debt. Which is why the limit has been increased 100 times. Each limit increase allowing for more spending and further increases in political power.

For the Left, leadership is considered a trusted wielding of great power by a *disinterested* bureaucrat or politician. Herbert Croly, the original editor of The Nation, a Leftist and Progressive magazine, said "The only entirely satisfactory solution of the difficulty is offered by the systematic authoritative transformation of the private interest of the individual into a disinterested devotion to a special object." (Croly, 1911, p. 418) The difficulty with this proposition, as James Buchanan has suggested with Public Choice, is that no politician is disinterested nor are some special set individual citizens or well-educated philosophers like Croly. Our self-interest is an important regulator of our lives and interactions. Indeed, our self-interest is our human common denominator which is preserved in history and law (English Common Law, the Code of Hammurabi, Magna Carta, etc), codified in the Ten Commandments and our consistent treatment of our fellow man: *do onto others and you would do onto yourself.* Self-interest, not selfish interest when considered across humanity is public virtue in a republic. Though Croly and many on the Left would dispatch self-interest in favor a disinterested leadership and electorate, the disinterested elite does not exist. A perfectly rational person would still need a subjective base of principles upon which to make decisions. According to Croly's self-interest, this perfect leader is guided principles of the Progressive philosophy whose rationale for existence is increasing the powerful political footprint of the Left. So much for a disinterested, altruistic leader. This disinterested group decided that borrowing $1 trillion in each of the last five years to cover their check-writing. So much for *disinterested!*

Croly's thinking was precisely the foundation thinking for most of our politicians and economists in the '30s through the '70s with few contrarians. When Buchanan proposed 'Politics without Romance' and 'Public Choice' the notion that the monies spent by Congress had value, political value, and therefore power worth trade, his ideas were not welcome on the Left. Per Buchanan:

> 'There is a familiar criticism of public choice theory to the effect that it is ideologically biased. In comparing and analyzing alternative sets of constitutional rules, both those in existence and those that might be introduced prospectively, how does public choice theory, as such, remain neutral in the scientific sense?

'Here it is necessary to appreciate the prevailing mindset of social scientists and philosophers at the midpoint of the 20th century when public choice arose. The socialist ideology was pervasive, and was supported by the allegedly neutral research programme called 'theoretical welfare economics', which concentrated on identifying the failures of observed markets to meet idealized standards. In sum, this branch of inquiry offered theories of market failure. But failure in comparison with what? The implicit presumption was always that politicized corrections for market failures would work perfectly. In other words, market failures were set against an idealized politics.

'Public choice then came along and provided analyses of the behavior of persons acting politically, whether voters, politicians or bureaucrats. These analyses exposed the essentially false comparisons that were then informing so much of both scientific and public opinion. In a very real sense, public choice became a set of theories of governmental failures, as an offset to the theories of market failures that had previously emerged from theoretical welfare economics. Or, as I put it in the title of a lecture in Vienna in 1978, public choice may be summarized by the three-word description, 'politics without romance'. (Buchanan, Public Choice: Politics Without Romance, 2003, Spring)

Much of the Leftist tradition of Roosevelt and Wilson is in full execution today. The left believes that a few special leaders can far more effectively navigate and order 'the general will' and our individual pursuit of happiness than we can execute on our own. If the last 80 years is testament to the Left's track record, then their economic, social and culture metrics show precisely the opposite. As noted on page 49, our social and financial indicators are down over the last several decades. A business with this kind of metrics would have already tanked and its leadership fired. In government, rent-seeking politicians navigate troubled finances by borrowing and spending more, writing more checks, collecting more votes and more political power.

The feedback loop of power and money vested in the political parties is one that President Washington worried about during his farewell address in 1796.

> "All obstructions to the execution of the laws, all combinations and associations, under whatever plausible character, with the real design to direct, control, counteract, or awe the regular deliberation and action of the constituted authorities, are destructive of this fundamental principle, and of fatal tendency. They serve to organize faction, to give it an artificial and extraordinary force; to put, in the place of the delegated will of the nation the will of a party, often a small but artful and enterprising minority of the community; and, according to the alternate triumphs of different parties, to make the public administration the mirror of the ill-concerted and incongruous projects of faction, rather than the organ of consistent and wholesome plans digested by common counsels and modified by mutual interests."

For Herbert Croly, Washington's words may ring deaf. It is *especially* delightful that Washington did not come by his wisdom at Harvard or Yale but from hard work and diligent reading and investigation of life itself. Washington, in fact, did not go to college. His wisdom was hard earned. He was not a disinterested intellectual. He was an interested American with specific values based on his Christian beliefs and his broad experience. His considered opinion about political power and its likely abuses is unexceptional in that one would expect this insight from a wise leader. Today this wisdom has not been heeded by any politician.

The power vested in the political parties, which, in the last election for each party equated to their $1 billion war chests stuffed full by of special interests from unions to businesses to a variety of social interests from Planned Parenthood to Right to Life organizations, is titanic. One billion dollars were spent by each party to assure the status quo during an election that should have debated our broken governance and enormous economic issues, a debate that should have discussed "wholesome plans digested by common counsels and modified by mutual interests." The election, though, was about each party retaining as much political power as possible. The result of the election was this: nothing happened.

Daniel Hennigner of the Wall Street Journal (1/3/2013) in the article *Repealing Reagan*, suggested after the passage of the American Taxpayer Relief Act of 2012 (an Act that purported to remedy of fiscal cliff dilemma) that our political interest groups and commercial interests 'swim through streams of revenue processed by the tax code out of the general fund and back to the favored fish.' Hennigner names a variety of special interest tax breaks for green projects all the way to Nascar that acquired tax breaks or tax credits from the Act. For all the weeks that Congress worked to stem the tide of debt, only $40-$60 billion a year in tax increases were trolled for tax relief and nearly $400 billion (over ten years) in spending increases. So the reform package that might reduce our overall debt, reform for which neither party has a constituency, found no traction, netted no spending reductions. The fish on both sides of the aisle will find that the worms they have feed their constituency will continue the expanding helix of power for which all will be kindly rewarded with – more power. Precisely.

Were there only a single reason to reduce the size of government it would be reduce to the amount of political donations chasing the status quo thus reducing the magnitude of power in our Capitol. Congress has tried to slow the funding mechanisms has been tried and tried and tried with no effect on the continuing spiral of political spending on campaign. And money is both power and speech, attempting to limit speech is not reasonable in a democracy.

The only way to limit the amount of money spent is to reduce the size of the government's footprint. The government is 'too big for its britches' and the parties to selfish in their intent to grow its size and their power.

Increased power in the federal government translates into reduced power for the states and our citizens. Whether our stories are like the Smith family or Mr. Zucker or just the average Joe trying to fill out an IRS 1040, we are increasingly at the mercy of a government and elected leaders, judicial, legislative and executive, that know no bounds for power.

Politicians' are always willing to talk in delightfully glittering generalities to get elected then kick problems down the road once elected. Both political parties are willing accomplices in managerial dysfunction. Both parties enjoy the riches and power associated with the status quo. Though few leaders, political, business or otherwise seek to tackle any big issues, Governors Chris Christie and Scott Walker are two notable exceptions, viewing the utter incompetence of both parties to put big ideas on the table to reform or transform our government is, in a word, shocking.

What is the cost of too much centralized power in the federal government, too much political greed in our elected officials? Run to its logical maximum, allowing government to absorb 100% of our means of production, then the cost is 100% of GDP. Government becomes 100% in charge and therefore 100% inefficient at managing our freedoms and resources. Examples include the Soviet Union, Cuba, Red China and the Pot Pol Government of Cambodia. In these countries citizens become totally disengaged, productivity is significantly defaced, and long term economic prospects move to zero. Though there were no political rent seekers in these countries, the government, through force, consumed 100% of the political power. These countries should have been the Left's shining examples of the perfection of disinterested leadership. Instead they are perfect examples of how central planning, as Hayek believed, were ineffective, and how great power, as Lord Acton stated, corrupts absolutely. Though never admitted or articulated, it is likely that even

Keynes would see total centralization as a very bad option. He was, afterall, according to himself, a capitalist. He just wanted to be in charge.

Between total centralization and America's growing centralization, a litany of poorly run leftist democracies stipple the world economy: Greece, Italy, Spain, Venezuela, Argentina, Ireland, France, and a litany of other including the former economic giant, Japan, who debt is over 200% of GDP.   Coming up to meet this litany of poor performance is America.

Political power has neutralized change in these countries much in the same way we are experiencing the rapid increase of government control here in America. At some point, when other countries stop buying our debt, and interest rates begin to rise. Quantitative easing will lose its appeal, and heavy regulation will provide no benefit. Washington's rent-seekers will have to get down to the hard work and difficult decisions they have ignored for decades. Government is not 'Just Right' and finding that balance will become a valued effort by the transformative political forces in America. Who are the transformers.   More later, but liberalism seems a great option.

Deficiency Eight: Complexity and Leftist Governance

Hernando de Soto's brilliant book The Mystery of Capital highlights a litany of legal complexities around that world, especially in third world and former communist nations, that inhibit the free exchange and ownership of property. Mr. de Soto estimates the complexity of laws that are barriers to ownership mean that about $9 trillion extralegal property cannot be leveraged as equity for new capital. If these nations could streamline the process for ownership and increase transparency purchase/sell transactions de Soto estimates that GDP growth in these countries could grow as high as 10%.

Property rights are one very important key to economic success. In many countries, the complexity of property law protects the landed to the exclusion of the landless, or for those who have lived on 'extra-legal' land for decades, the title-less. Many citizens simply squat on property in lieu of attempting to endure the hardship of legally acquiring the land which make take years and tens or hundreds to legal steps. These arduous legal steps help lawyers to protect the landed but assure that free and reasonable exchange of title for new ownership is all but impossible. Per de Soto:

'In Haiti, one way an ordinary citizen can settle legally on government land is first to lease it from the government for five years and then buy it. Working with associates in Haiti, our researchers found that to obtain such a least took 65 bureaucratic steps – requiring, on average, a little more than two years – all for the privilege of merely leasing the land for five years. To buy the land required another 111 bureaucratic hurdles – and twelve more years. Total time to gain lawful land in Haiti: nineteen years. … In fact, in every country we investigated, we found that it is very nearly as difficult to stay legal as it is to become legal.' (Soto, The Mystery of Capital, 2000, p. 4)

Complexity is the mother of inefficiency and in this case a killer of the golden goose: capital. Although much blame can be laid at the feet of the culture of government, the history and traditions of how one governs, the author understands that lawyers, whether legislative or commercial, help incur extralegal activity:

> 'The difficulty is that few lawyers understand the economic consequences of their work, and their knee-jerk reaction to extra-legal behavior to large-scale change is generally hostile. All the reformers I have met working to make property more accessible to the poor operate with the presumption that the legal profession is their natural enemy. Economists involved in reform have become so frustrated with legal conservatism that they have invested time and money to discredit the legal profession. Using economic data from fifty-two countries from 1960 to 1980, Samar K Datta and Jeffrey B. Nugent have shown that over every percentage point increase in the number of lawyers in the labor force (from, say 0.5 to 1/5 percent), economic growth is reduced by 4.76 to 3.68 percent, this showing that economic growth is inversely related to the prudence of lawyers." (Soto, The Mystery of Captal, 2000, p. 10)

Lawyers aren't so much the bad guys, just myopic enablers of Progressive legislators, building dysfunctional monopolies and legal edifices whose command and control organizations are run by more lawyers. Legislation, instead of having the economy and dynamism of the language found in the Bill of Rights or Constitution, is more like a giant legal mote built to protect a castle (government monopoly) with legal strictures that require and mandate barriers to success for citizens or sovereign states, providing little or no flexibility for freedom for the individual or innovation by the State.

Worse, whether by habit or tradition, creation of regulatory or social policy tends to mimic criminal law. In criminal statutes it is necessary to specifically state each and every possible behavior that is illegal to assure that the judge and jury understand what is against the law so a criminal does not skate. When setting up a social agency or social policy, an endless outline of do's and don'ts create complexity and handcuffs innovation and precipitates expense. Though it is a very long road to tyranny, despotism or totalitarianism, the road along the way is harsh.

Lawyers are not the problem, but their tendency to complexity is just a symptom of a greater problem: the inability of legislators and president to understand problems well enough to articulate a simple solution. According to Albert Einstein, "If you cannot explain it simply, you do not understand it well enough." Poor problem-solving leads to complex, expensive, micro-managed solutions, generally in the form of a government monopoly. Two great examples, though wildly different in political execution, have had similarly poor effects on the economy: Obamacare and Sarbanes-Oxley.

Power-enabled passage of the Obamacare produced legislation rammed through a Democrat Controlled Congress, with only Democrats votes (219-213 – only one Republican vote), in the middle of night, almost exclusively done behind closed doors, even to the exclusion of a reading of the final document by most, if any, Democrats. At least Sarbanes-Oxley was a collaborative effort by Democrats and Republicans (vote tally - 423-3) after the telecom meltdown of 2003. The former is so politically over-reaching that 26 states challenged its Constitutionality. The later, though passed with bipartisan support, has managed to endure a continual harangue from business and liberal economists alike. Both add an unneeded level of complexity to already over-regulated markets.

As an example, here is a small chunk of text from Sarbanes Oxley, a surprisingly short 100 page document.

"(a) PROHIBITED ACTIVITIES- Section 10A of the Securities Exchange Act of 1934   (15 U.S.C. 78j-1) is amended by adding at the end the following:

(g) PROHIBITED ACTIVITIES- Except as provided in subsection (h), it shall be unlawful for a registered public accounting firm (and any associated person of   that firm, to the extent determined appropriate by the Commission) that   performs for any issuer any audit required by this title or the rules of the Commission under this title or, beginning 180 days after the date of commencement of the operations of the Public Company Accounting Oversight Board established under section 101 of the Sarbanes-Oxley Act of 2002 (in this section referred to as the `Board'), the rules of the Board, to provide to that issuer, contemporaneously with the audit, any non-audit service,

including--

`(1) bookkeeping or other services related to the accounting records or financial statements of the audit client;

`(2)   financial   information   systems   design   and implementation;

`(3) appraisal or valuation services, fairness opinions, or contribution-in-kind reports;

`(4) actuarial services;

`(5) internal audit outsourcing services;

`(6) management functions or human resources;

`(7) broker or dealer, investment adviser, or investment banking services;

`(8) legal services and expert services unrelated to the audit; and

`(9) any other service that the Board determines, by regulation, is impermissible. " (Sarbanes-Oxley)

This unneeded legislation is indeed criminal law, not a palliative for better accounting. Our nation's legislature didn't need to remedy fraudulent relationships between Accounting and Audit firms and their clients, so much as adjudicate on laws already on the books. But our legal concessionaires found that inaction did not play well in a political world. Sarbanes-Oxley, whose efficacy has been in question for as long as is existence, has had the unintended consequence of reducing the number of Initial Public Offerings by two-thirds in the United States over the last decade. In 'Where Have All the IPOs Gone, by Goa and Ritter:

> 'During 1980-2000, an average of 311 companies per year went public in the U.S. Since the technology bubble burst in 2000, the average has been only 102 initial public offerings (IPOs) per year, with the drop especially precipitous among small firms. Many have blamed the Sarbanes-Oxley Act of 2002 and the 2003 Global Settlement's effects on analyst coverage for the decline in IPO activity. We offer an alternative explanation. We posit that the advantages of selling out to a larger organization, which can speed a product to market and realize economies of scope, have increased relative to the benefits of operating as an independent firm.' (Xiaohui Gao, 2013)

The authors propose that IPOs flagged because companies could more easily sell to a larger corporation, but the fact that the cost of Sarbanes is high is not well considered. CRA International's survey of costs found that the typical small firms (under $700M) 'annual costs were around $2 million a year, and larger companies' costs exceeded $10 million.' (CRA International, 2006)

The ultimate result of Sarbox is that the poorly conceived and expensive legislation caught zero bad guys. The 2002 legislation missed a litany of bad guys including the infamous Bernie Madoff or Bernie Ebers. It certainly didn't help prevent the misdeeds of Freddie Mac and Fannie Mae encouraging sub-prime mortgages, or rating agencies like Moodys and S&P from providing good ratings for mortgage backed security. Sarbox did create a lot of paper work but not much value. The legislation did indeed do harm to thousands of publically-traded companies with millions of dollars of overhead and reporting to the government. Not to mention the potential costs to all the firms that did not attempt an IPO because of the harsh reporting requirements added to public firms.

The Sarbanes' creators look like pikers compared to the complexity created by a Democrat Congress dedicated to complexity perhaps like no other Congress, for they preceded Obamacare with 2000 pages of Cap and Trade and followed it with another 2000 pages of Dodd-Frank. Though Republicans have passed their share of complex and onerous legislation, the Democrats are the professionals of complexity.

Below is a second example of criminal style legalese is applied to creating a government monopoly. This is from Obamacare:

322

HR 3590 EAS/PP

1) "(b) SHARED RESPONSIBILITY PAYMENT.—

2) "(1) IN GENERAL.—If an applicable individual

3) fails to meet the requirement of subsection (a) for 1

4) or more months during any calendar year beginning

5) after 2013, then, except as provided in subsection (d),

6) there is hereby imposed a penalty with respect to the

7) individual in the amount determined under sub

8) section (c). (Representatives, 2009)

The paragraphs before these words from the Healthcare Act defend the right of this legislation to regulate this mandate as commerce, that is per the act: "section referred to as the "requirement" is commercial and economic in nature, and substantially affects interstate commerce, as a result of the effects described in paragraph (2)." Pages of legalese were inserted to protect this monopoly from legal assault – i.e. the lawyers took the time to defend creating a set of mandates – inside the act itself? Perhaps, regarding the Constitutionality of their writings, their level of confidence must have been down a bit that day. Regardless, this mandate should get under any citizen's skin, but this is just the type of the problem with Obamacare. This document is 2409 pages long.

Setting up a monopoly that mandates that 47 million people to purchase insurance, it appears, is not just complex. It is shocking complex.

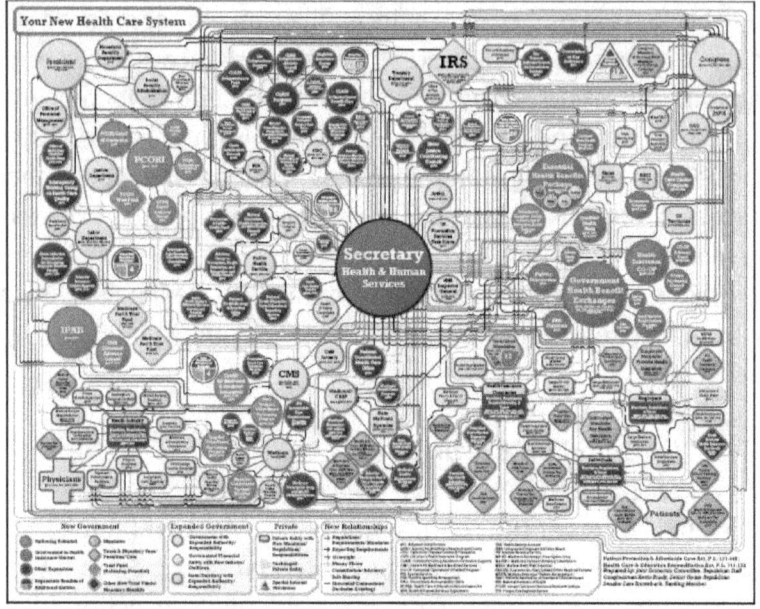

Figure: Obamacare Organization Chart (The Daily Bail, 2012)

Reading though the chart is a bit difficult. Without any reading, consider how well any company might fare if its organizational chart looked like this. The images's plethora of lines and shapes shows 68 grant programs, 47 bureaucratic entities, 29 demonstration projects, 6 regulatory bodies, 6 compliance standards and 2 entitlements. Importantly, it allots Health and Human Services Secretary, Kathleen Sebelius, and any of her progeny, near dictatorial power with no Congressional oversight. The law has 2200 references and 600 new authorities that cannot be challenged. It's a bit shocking, frankly, that even the Left would be so negligent to give so much power to one person and completely ignore the merits of the balance of power so diligently written into our Constitution. But, lawyers, once engaged, take the building of the mote around their health finance castle very seriously. But the 2000 plus pages were only a starting point for further regulation. Sebelius and drew have had to complete the law with additional rules and regulations. The tome now stretches to 10,516 pages, eight times the length of the Bible. (Star, 2013)

Reviewing the ABOVE chart again and again, it would appear that Einstein, and his notions about simplicity, was not invited to this legislative rules writing party. Simplicity was not the mission of the legislators. Einstein would likely suggest that the legal engineers on this project did not really understand the problem, or more perfectly, or in everyday language, they could not see the forest for the trees.

When Isaac Newton looked up in the sky at night and saw millions and millions of stars, he could have produced a chart much like the one above, with stars placed nicely in a grid. He could have drawn lines and named Constellations as the ancients did. But he didn't. He discovered there was an underlying description of how matter, on heaven and earth, acted. The result of understanding the problem: he calculated that gravity had a simple relationship: $F = Gm_1m_2/r^2$. It's a simple law that defines the force of gravity between two objects, any two objects. Tragically, the legal counterparts in Washington could not see the simplicity of the health market, only the complexity of the enforcement mechanisms and the invention of bureaucratic committees to assure the mandates are met. What are the likely results? This from Forbes Magazine via the CBO.

"Today, the Congressional Budget Office announced the results of a new analysis of the Affordable Care Act's individual mandate, the law's provision that forces Americans to buy health insurance or face a fine. According to CBO, 11-12 million uninsured Americans will be subject to the mandate; the agency expects more than half of them to pay the fine instead of buying insurance. But there's something that the CBO didn't say: as more people pay the "tax penalty" instead of buying insurance, premiums for everyone else will go up, potentially triggering a death spiral in the private insurance market." (Roy, CBO: 11 Million Uninsured Americans Will Be Subject to Obamacare's Individual Mandate 'Penalty Tax', 2012)

Interestingly Obamacare will effect only 11-12 million uninsured Americans, though there are nearly 47 million – the original target of the legislation. The result is that a government monopoly set up in the dark of night behind closed doors so that 47 million citizens would have access to health financing, will a very large cohort of the intended population and ultimately cause a *death spiral* in the fully functioning private healthcare financing market place. Other problems exist as well. The states received the power to ignore the government mandate via the Supreme Court's finding in the summer of 2012. The court found that the mandate was instead a tax, but also gave states the right to reject a mandate to setup healthcare exchanges, nor do the states have to expand Medicaid rolls as mandated as well. This illustrates another disadvantage of too much power vested in one group, in this case the Democrat Party. The bill was rushed and not well written. Nancy Pelosi further indicts herself and the Democrats regarding the competence of their work. "We have to pass the bill so you can find out what is in it"

For American citizens, our power is diminished by the increasing amount of dollars taken from our wallets and by having options only to vote for two Parties whose mission is to maintain the status quo.

The financial cliff we are heading for is vastly more treacherous than the one navigated at the beginning of 2013 by Obama and Speaker Boehner. At the beginning of the 20th century the Federal government consumed 2.5% of GDP, with the states and local government combining for just under 5%. Today the federal government is devouring 24.5% (2012) of power of our nation, with state and local government requiring another 21%, four percent of the 21% from federal mandates. The real numbers are more like 28.5% for the Feds and 17% for the local and state. As the federal government grows to 40% of GDP, what power is left for the state, localities and the citizens is abating at an alarming rate.

The Left has produced a culture of governance whose organizational structure has great power, but lackluster results. Too much power in the federal government has not produced elegance or simplicity but more complexity, expense, misallocation of resources, and an ever expanding double helix of poor performance from poor problem-solving. Power, too much power, is the corrupting influence, one that the Founding Father's tried to protect us from by creating a limited federal government.

Regarding complexity, there is little research that complexity in any solution is an optimal managerial, organizational or scientific solution. The body of work surrounding simplicity is, however, voluminous and a tradition for centuries from Aristotle's "We consider it a good principle to explain the phenomena by the simplest hypothesis possible." To Occam's Razor: 'simpler explanations are, other things being equal, generally better than more complex ones. To the KISS principle, Keep It Simple Stupid. When nearly every sensible person works to simplify our government and a legion of lawyers are going in precisely the opposite direction.

"When I'm working on a problem, I never think about beauty. I think only how to solve the problem. But when I have finished, if the solution is not beautiful, I know it is wrong." - R. Buckminster Fuller (1895 - 1983), American Architect, Author, Designer, Inventor, and Futurist

The Left has an entirely different view. "There is always an easy solution to every human problem - neat, plausible, and wrong." - H.L. Mencken (1880 - 1956), American Journalist, Essayist, and Editor.

The costs of this complexity may be measurable as an additional factor to the costs of managing social programs noted earlier but is not in the scope or capabilities of this author. Consider that Americans waste 6.1 billion hours doing taxes. (Novac, 2011) With America's median family income at around $55,000 a year ($27.50 an hour), the dollar value of this waste is about $160 billion, or about 1% of GDP. Add in Sarbanes, EPA and EEOC rules for

Business, and a flurry of other government rules and regulation, they pop the ever complex Obamacare on top, as estimate of 3% is fairly easy to reach.

Deficiency Nine: Success without Failure

To avoid or allay failure in all facets of life, private and public, personal and government, all but assures a moderation or extinction of success. When government either ignores failures or creates controls to extinguish either its own failure or failure in the economy or society in general, mediocrity or worse is sure to follow.

Imagine if our families worked like government, setting up a safety net for all possible eventualities, to assure that failure was simply not possible. Families that over nurture and over protect do not produce the world's most productive new citizens. And imagine the expense. Additional insurance, extra protective barriers for children and adults, hedge funds to protect against job loss. But most of us know this as a matter of common knowledge and common sense that these are fools missions. We know taking a bit of risk is a good thing. As Arthur Brooks suggested earlier success is earned by hard work, by taking risks and many times by failing, then finding a new path to success. This true of our personal lives, for well-run businesses and for government. Failure is an essential component of success.

The federal government and those our leaders who management its policy, though, spend vast resources to assure that failure is erased from the human equation. It is our federal creed for social policy via redistribution of wealth, central social planning via acquisition of our personal responsibilities with federal mandates like Medicare and Obamacare, and in economics via crony capitalism.

What intellectual habit creates the economic mindset that minimizing competition is beneficial to the economy? What creative economic theory suggests that government ownership of businesses, like GM and Chrysler during the 2008 meltdown is optimal use of economic resources? What odd notion is required to believe that absorbing our personal responsibilities will enhance our lives? All of these perceived duties of our government, though, do in fact reduce competition and the possibility of failure. These bad mental habits show up in our personal lives where our children play a game without keeping score or attend a school where grading success in considered passé.

In a socialist regime these ideas are greeted happily. Government protection from failure is readily accepted. So, for instance, the major reform, Dodd Frank, passed after the 2008 economic meltdown, assured that large banks, banks that are too big to fail, are now regulated in a way that produces a market that favors them because of their size.   The legislation builds an uneven playing field for large banks to compete against smaller banks, and then assures if failure occurs that the government will be there with a check.   If banks are too big to fail, then perhaps regulation that split up banks into smaller commercial and retail, a Glass-Stegall approach might prove more effective and more competitive.   As for GM and Chrysler would have benefited greatly from an orderly private bankruptcy without government interference.   The premises of our social welfare system is entirely build on the notion that government should assure that no one should be susceptible to economic failure – that a government debit card is always available at the moment personal success expires and that debit card is available in perpetuity.   The point, though, is clear.   If success is best optimized because failure is a possibility, then the state should not be a vessel of assurances against failure, but a progression of solutions that create success.   Failure should be an accepted path for attaining success, not a path to be avoided at all costs.

Steve Jobs is a great example of why failure is so important in our lives.   Jobs is remembered as a great entrepreneur, the guy that started a company in his garage that grew to a corporate giant.   We remember the guy that came back to Apple when its finances and failures were plummeting and how he saved the company with the iPod, iPhone and iPad. What we don't see in jobs are failures.

Nick Shultz, writing in the National Review, had quite a different and important view of Mr. Jobs. He said 'Jobs failed better than anyone else in Silicon Valley, maybe better than anyone in corporate America.   By that I mean Jobs did what only the greatest entrepreneurs can do: learn from their failures. I don't mean learn from their mistakes. I mean learn from their abject, humiliating, bonehead, epic fails.' (Schultz, 2011)   What is seldom talked about Jobs' abject failure at NeXT Computers or the number of failures that were likely required to produce that first Apple, the first iPod and the products that Jobs conceived that never made it to market.

Shultz continues: 'There's a moral here for a Washington culture that fears failure too much. In today's Washington, large banks aren't permitted to fail; nor are large auto firms. Next up will be too-big-to-fail hospital systems. Steve Jobs is a reminder that failure is a good and necessary thing. And that sometimes the greatest glories are born of catastrophe.'

Shultz is onto something. Failure is an essential component for success, for greatness. Our worst American Tragedy is when risk, failure and opportunity are excised from every level of our culture from 'banks too big to fail' to our children's' sports events where no score is kept. No success or failure, just esteem building.

For Washington's leader, more time should be spent figuring out how Steve Jobs created jobs and less time on a safety net that deprives citizens, business and our civil society of both success and failure.

Deficiency Ten: The Cultural Pillars of Leftist Democracy

The problem-solving tools of the Left are based on the cultural notions that form the foundation of their thinking: centralized power, rational thinking without content or faith, equality in all things, and economic justice. Building with these tools, the results have produced social monopolies, complexity, federal power consumption, and command and control philosophy based on micro-managing some facet of social, economic or political policy. As the goal of the Left has been to create great society, the results have been tragically wanting. Their scorecard for failure:

- 40% illegitimacy rate (60% marriage rate) up from 4% in 1950
- Education competency flat despite 200% increase in real spending over 30 years
- 900% decline in savings rate over 60 years
- Financially unsustainable Retirement System (health and pension) $45T unfunded mandate
- Very high jobless rate 7.9% for February 2013 (11.7% including those who have ceased to look for work and those who have chosen to acquire the disability route)
- National debt exceeds 100% of GDP, increasing rapidly
- A rising tide of social monopolies the strip nearly 10% of our economic efficiency

If adding to government spending (24.2% of GDP) and adding more government monopolies to their power base is useful in creating economic success, then Obama's economic policies should have, according to Keynesian Economics, produced a vastly better economy than President Clinton, who with a Republican Congress had reduced spending to 18.1% of GDP and bore significantly lower debt.

The Left's cultural pillars are taking America down an economic, social and cultural road which leaves government larger and more controlling and with its citizens keeping less of their wealth and liberties. This shift from our traditional cultural pillars has a direct and debilitative effect on our understanding of the Constitutional, how we legislate, and the ultimate diminution of the thriving American Society, Culture and Economy.

The net effect is, as we have the fewer freedoms, our chances for personal or national greatness are eroded. The cultural pillars of a liberal democracy are quite the opposite of the Lefts: decentralization of power, liberty as the catalyst of individual greatness, hard work, and faith with reason. The question is not whether the Left's pillars of governance effective at creating great results. They do not. The question is 'what is the rule or measure of governance that helps its citizens understand when government grows too big and powerful and begins to harm its citizens.' Today, no measure exists and this may be the greatest deficiency of all. When there is no measure of success, the citizen is held captive by political greed in search of the status quo.

Summary

More deficiencies are available for discussion such as government investment in businesses, lack of best practices for running its organizations, and the unionization of federal employees, but the objective of this book is to keep it short and to point, the most important points.

The Left's cultural pillars have proven incapable of organizing big government solutions that produce great results. As noted on the previous page, results have not been great, moderate, or average. Results have been exceedingly poor, with every social and economic indicator having diminished over the last 80 years.

A negative attitude about the abilities of its citizens has produced an endless array of regulations to protect us from ourselves (i.e. like the demise of the 100 watt light bulb) and growing base of government monopolies that dispense goods and services without regard to burgeoning costs. Rent-seeking by our legislators has produced the fuel by which government continues on its rapid growth pace with no judicial, legislative or presidential throttle for the exploding power base in Washington. Complaints from citizens about election spending have been answered with regulation (McCain-Feingold) that allows even more dollars to be spent, increasing the rent-seeking. The continuing spiral downward is fueled by money assuring the status quo, more monopolies which require more federal spending and taxes, and the need for more power for the political elites which is never fully sated.

About the only good that can be retrieved from our current state of governance is that though the leaders' intentions seem to be well-intentioned, their execution leaves much to be desired.

THE EFFICIENCIES OF A LIMITED FEDERAL GOVERNMENT

Since the beginning of time, a powerful central government was the only form of government. Governments existed via divine right or through ruthless employment of force, or in many cases both. For centuries the common man lived by feast or famine, war or peace, but seldom had enough control of his destiny to achieve more than basic subsistence. Liberal Democracy exploded into existence in 1789 in America, and though although Democracy has fared well since, Liberalism has not. Politics has diminished Liberalism in America and around the world in favor of another version of strong central government which replaces the Devine Right of Kings and Dictators with the Rational Mandate from the Left for Big Government.

Liberal Democracy, invented in America and tested to a lesser degree in parliamentary has now been on the wane in America and around the world debilitated by the onslaught of the Left over the last 80 years. Liberal governance has existed only as a tiny branch on the constant tree of strong central government, a sidebar to history. It successes, however, are not difficult to measure and catalog. In America the results of the Great Experiment in Liberal Democracy produced history's most phenomenal economic, social and cultural results. There are no peers. American Liberalism's emphasis on a lean government with limited powers proved to be one crucial tenet for individual success. Spreading power between federal branches and to states and its citizens moderated corrupting power in the center. Giving great power and great freedom to citizens first tested whether liberty was indeed the engine of success then confirmed it as America became the economic engine of the world over the course of its first 150 years. Now the test is different. At what tipping point does government power clip our individual paths to greatness, reducing the potential both of the individual and the nation?

Though the Constitution specifies no correct percentage for the size of government and there shouldn't be one, the Constitution allows for flexibility. In times of war the size and spending of government soars and during economic growth spurts the size may diminish slightly. Yet finding a reasonable metric or measure for an effective balance between what is too large or too small is crucial to long term success of our nation. The success in sizing government begins with understanding how government views its citizens, and how this view affects the role of government and therefore its girth. The Left's pessimistic view necessarily requires a large, vigilant government spreading wealth and regulating conduct, mandating outcomes. A Liberal, optimistic view understands that people are vessels of greatness that need freedom to execute personal, shared and corporate visions and require little guidance or help in finding their road to greatness.

Liberal governance's view of the human condition must be built upon a coalition of ideas to succeed, among them:

- a general optimism of an individual's ability to seek and fulfill a better life for himself and his family
- that rights are provided to humanity, not by government, but prior to the existence of government, from God and Nature,
- that the greatness of our nation is built from the bottom up, with the individual being the cornerstone of a great society, economy and culture, and
- that government that should no more than is minimally required, and when testing solutions outside its responsibility must employ very high measures of success for continuation of any solution.

Without these basic beliefs Liberalism deteriorates into the pessimism of big government. *Efficiencies* will focus on how to use the cultural pillars of governance: liberty, decentralized government, hard work and faith with reason as tools for creating policy, programs, and legislation.

Assuring an individual's success is the most important responsibility of government, and the Declaration of Independence lays the groundwork for this requirement with these simply words: 'We hold these truths to be self-evident, that all men are created equal, that they are endowed by their Creator with certain unalienable Rights, that among these are Life, Liberty and the pursuit of Happiness.--That to secure these rights, Governments are instituted among Men, deriving their just powers from the consent of the governed.'

How does a Liberal Government efficiently provide for the success of each man?   By understanding what building blocks are essential for personal success.   As we have seen the Left's approach with government monopolies, complex laws, onerous regulation and forced equality have had a negative impact on our nation and especially those in most need. What basic axioms of human nature and human success which are essential to building a great life? What should government protect at all costs?   What institutions should every man and women participate that produces a satisfying and valuable life?   What institutions build a strong economic, social, spiritual and culture life.

Four valued social traditions have consistently beat the test of time and, regardless of geography or faith or race, these nucleotides for success work:

- Get an education and continue to educate oneself throughout life
- Work hard and if one job does not satisfy one's economic needs, work harder
- Get married, stay married, and build a durable emotional relationship that will last a lifetime
- Join and faith community or civic organization and participate in a mission that is greater than your life

Though measuring government success will be discussed later, these four building blocks are also the Key Process Indicators that measure not only individual success, but social and cultural health of our nation. Leftist will agree with these KPI's but only to the degree that government can directly affect them. Education means government schools. Hard work is accomplished only by government dictat. Marriage is not central to a man and woman and child, but any arrangement with a child. And faith is something that must be tolerated.

In a Liberal Democracy, government's responsibility is not so much to foster each of these but to assure in the course of its responsibilities that government does no harm. Inevitably government will experiment and government will as often do harm to these very important building blocks. A great Liberal government will understand its mistakes and reform itself. Leftist governments are not good at admitting mistakes and frankly almost any government is very poor at reviewing its maladies.

When Liberal government exists only by the consent of the governed, then citizens must have tools to measure government success. The final section of Efficiencies will recommend several metrics that citizens should use evaluate the quality of our governed and to give consent, our vote, for the continued residency in Washington for our leaders.

As an additional note, the book will not delve deeply into the Western and Protestant belief that God is a loving and forgiving. This view of forgiving God is new and vastly different than the much less forgiving God's of Old Testament Christian, Jewish and Moslem history that were historically used to keep the non-elites in their place. Hell, fire and damnation are prizes for leaders without competence whose modern rendition is found in socialists' rational mandate of government and the 'general will.' Without Liberalism's more optimistic conception of God, a God that loves, forgives and redeems His Fallen flock, liberalism could not easily exist. A deeper discussion of Faith as a pillar of Liberal Governance can be found in *Irreconcilable Differences* by this author.

On the Condition of Man: Liberalism's View of Humanity

As history proceeded through the Reformation and Renaissance, the growing belief that all men were capable of reasonable and successful lives, not just the inner circle of Monarchists and Tyrants, the notion of a Republic gained favor, and then, finally, in America a new more hopeful form of government flourished, Federalism and Liberal democracy. That all men were created equally by God, translated into a simple optimism: that though man is fallen, all men's capabilities to climb the ladder of greatness, is directly connected liberty, to his or her freedom when disconnected from the chains of government. Liberalism success is individual success, success accessible by every free man and women. Without faith that all mankind, not just the few, can and will accept the challenge and hardship of life, liberal democracy would be at odds with any conception of government. Christ's simple words, 'Forgive them, Father, for they know not what they do,' changed the world. These words intone a hopeful spirit unknown to mankind. Forgiveness and tolerance, allow us to fail, then succeed as better people, better citizens, better moms and dads, workers and employers. Success is a long road in life, and failure is just a rung on the ladder, a lesson that helps make us better.

The Left's pessimism of man is characterized by its micromanagement of social and economic policy, and its complete divergence from the notion of Natural Rights. With little or no faith that mankind can fend for himself, any government will grasp more and more power to control its populations and will ultimately veer toward tyranny, toward a government requiring increasing control of the affairs of its citizens. When strong, central government misunderstands how to effectively deploy sound social and economic policy, three classes form. In America, these classes are becoming very well defined 1) the political elites, 2) the haves, and 3) a permanent underclasses.

But more than Liberal optimism in man's abilities is required to produce a government that will endure. Federal leadership must be vigilant to assure a trusted relationship between the governed and government. This trusted relationship is bolstered when the government understands that its fundamental responsibility is protecting our rights. Rights are owned by citizens, not government, and given to us God and Nature. This is a crucial differentiator from Left and Liberal, and an essential building block for great governance and leadership. When citizens allow their elected leaders to believe that government dispenses rights, the road from Liberalism is a short trip to a soft tyranny, and then a more terrible tyranny.

Leaders that understand their ability to lead is built upon the same rights its citizens enjoy also understand the humble basis for our existence with God and Nature. There is no room for political elites in a Liberal democracy. For the Left, though, humility is not part of their Progressive Leader. This fact is easily on display with not only the Democrat leaders in office today, but is most assuredly missing in many of the inhabitants on the other side of the political aisle as well. When government becomes the adversary of our individual freedoms, it is at war was its citizens. Leadership flags and then becomes protective of poor results. Government inaction follows and stasis results. As we see in our current situation, our nation has come to a social, economic and cultural halt.

Over the last 80 years our Left-leaning government has dispensed new *rights* via social entitlements. By any standard of Liberal governance, government may not be the giver of rights. Programs like Social Security or Welfare are not rights or entitlements, but gifts or privileges. Rights cannot be given or taken away by the government and maintain its Liberal footing. That FDR and LBJ and Obama have managed to create new privileges does not mean there approach is right only that our legislative, executive and judicial leaders have lost faith in the traditional pillars of governance and in liberalism itself. Why? As von Hayek proposed when asked why Keynesianism so flourished among economists, he answered that perhaps they liked the *control* the theories gave them. When rights are dispensed by government, control by government increases, its power increases and then creates a feedback loop through public choice/rent-seeking that creates more government and more centralization of power. A key measure of great, liberal leadership, is built on a willingness of elected officials push power and responsibility out to states and American citizens.

For Liberalism to thrive our rights must be protected by government not dispensed by government. When the political class understands that its citizens are the root of national success and humbly protect our rights and freedoms, only then can America return to liberalism and access our on ramp to greatness.

This bears reemphasizing: The founding father's believed that every single person on earth is born with rights which include life, liberty and pursuit of happiness. They also understood that additional rights described in the Bill of Rights belong solely to individuals and should never be diminished by government. Never. This is a core pillar of Liberalism and American Liberal governance which has not been duplicated as fully by any other government since the writing of the Constitution. There is no country on earth where individual rights, so broad and wide, have been published, ratified and then protected by government. Said another way, the America Constitution and Bill of Rights are the most Liberal social contracts in history.

Keynes noted that the masses were too ignorant, too unenlightened, to act in the public interest. To say this point of view is arrogant and *unenlightened* is understatement. Though it is unlikely individuals make conscious decisions based on some grand intellectual scheme called public interest, their self-interest almost uniformly and collectively results in a well-ordered social environment because chaos is not in our self-interest. Our self-interest keeps us inside the lines on the freeway and close to the speed limit because getting killed isn't a good option. We generally do not buy a bad product twice, forcing the manufacturer to improve or go out of business. We negotiate price when we can, and when we sell something, even at a garage sale, we allow prices to float to assure maximum sales. In general, people act wisely, because it is in their best interest. When these common activities are done as a collection of national events, this collection of people seeking better lives and who are in the pursuit of happiness, create a great nation.

The conceit of Keynes, Croly, Rousseau, Marx and Obama is that they believe they are wiser than us, that the enlightened class, whoever they may be, can better organize our lives than we can, that our Liberties must be organized and controlled for us, for our own good and which can be over ruled by the state when in the best interest of the state. There is no example of an increasingly-centralized state that produces perpetual and widespread prosperity. Conversely, a government that assures our rights by building simple legal foundations upon which we compete for opportunities ultimately maximizes our freedoms *and* opportunities. In the world's one Liberal Democracy, ours, this foundation produced not only the greatest economy in the world, but the greatest society and culture as well.

As America has slid from our Liberal foundation of greatness, however, our nation foundered. "What is the most effective size of government if the current rendition is becoming overbearing and, the original social contract, the Articles of Confederation, was too weak?' In our transition from the 'Articles,' to Federalism, to Leftist Democracy, our political leaders have turned from public servants to kings and barons. The political elites seek more to extend their political livelihoods than propound our freedoms.

John Locke proposed that Kings had no special rights or gifts with simple logic. If we all descended from Adam and Adam had no special right to leadership and had to count on God for his existence, then Kings were not divine and thus lead only by power and force, not from God's divination of corporal power. Conversely, if Adam did enjoy divine right, then so must us all.

'All these premises having, as I think, been clearly made out, it is impossible that the rulers now on earth should make any benefit, or derive any the least shadow of authority from that, which is held to be the fountain of all power, Adam's private dominion and paternal jurisdiction; so that he that will not give just occasion to think that all government in the world is the product only of force and violence, and that men live together by no other rules but that of beasts, where the strongest carries it, and so lay a foundation for perpetual disorder.' (Locke, Second Treatise of Government, 2011, p. 3)

The Left has produced our nation's new kings and dictators. Liberal optimism about man and fundamental tenet that our rights are equally given to all – kings, political elites, and us -produces only one class of which we all belong. To climb back onto our Liberal mountain, leadership needs many important qualities. Virtue tops that list. Montesquieu believed that for a Republic to be effective it leaders required virtue.

'When virtue is banished ambition invades the minds of those who are disposed to receive it, and avarice possesses the whole community. The objects of their desires are changed; what they were fond of before is become indifferent; they were free while under the restraint of laws, but they would fain now be free to act against law;' (Charles de Secondat, 2011, Locations 1189-1191)

It is hard to imagine such prescience about our condition of government today, from a man that died over 260 years ago. Our leaders today should draw on this wisdom because very many have lost their understanding of how to lead well and with virtue. As a result, instead of leaders of a noble republic, they act more like monarchs or despots, who have lost their honor. Virtue understands clearly that greatness is not built on the backs of those who lead, but created by those who understand how to enable citizens' abilities and assure their rights.

If the foundations of Liberal government are based on our inviolable rights given by God and Nature, and optimism about man's capabilities, then the need for micro-management of our lives, the need for government monopolies to dispense faux rights, and the requirement for complexity to address hundreds of millions of person issues, falls away. Trusting our fellow man with so many freedoms is a very tough road for the political elite to ride upon. Trust is difficult but necessary. Trust, though, is essential to our success as a nation, personally, corporately and politically. Trust is an essential virtue upon with a great society it built. Trust is a two-way street. When government power grows, the trust of the governed becomes skeptical.

Constraining the size of government is only part of the answer to restraining the power of government. A small government can be just as onerous as the ever-growing, centralized government like the Leviathan in Washington today. Regulation, like Dodd-Frank or Sarbanes-Oxley is just as debilitating to the economy whether the government consumes 25% of GDP (under Obama) or for that matter 10% (at some point in the future when Liberalism makes a comeback.) This approach to government begins with a pessimistic view of man and the need to regulate his existence. Breaking the government of the inefficient habits of creating more government, more monopolies and onerous regulations is an important step, but more is required to create operational excellence. Believing individual liberty is the primary superstructure for building policy and legislation is crucial to the culture of governance. Understanding that empowering individual is essential to building a great society is fundament to liberalism. But just as important, once any legal structure is created, conceiving and improving best practices is vital to good government as well. Quality process improvement is essential reducing costs. Testing new ideas is fundamental to any organization, but testing has to be combined with faithful measurements for success and a willingness to know when something has not met the American measure of greatness. Mediocre is not a reasonable outcome.

America's leaders must believe in freedom as a solution - that liberty, decentralized power, hard work and faith and reason are essential tools for building solutions. Full faith to these pillars is essential to creating a Liberal, vibrant America. Testing new ideas, though, is essential to identifying those things that are at odds with our personal success, but care must to taken to assure that our personal success built on centuries of wise tradition should never be hampered with.

Locke's insight regarding the importance of tradition in the building a government is exemplified in a letter to a friend in Paris during the French Revolution. This very bloody revolution meant to excise everything that pre-existed, leaving only an empty shell to build from.

'"The same policy pervades all the laws which have since been made for the reservation of our liberties. In the 1st of William and Mary, in the famous statute called the Declaration of Right, the two Houses utter not a syllable of "a right to frame a government for themselves." You will see that their whole care was to secure the religion, laws, and liberties that had been long possessed, and had been lately endangered. "Taking into their most serious consideration the *best* means for making such an establishment that their religion, laws, and liberties might not be in danger of being again subverted," they auspicate all their proceedings by stating as some of those *best* means, "in the *first place*," to do "as their *ancestors in like cases have usually* done for vindicating their *ancient* rights and liberties, 'to *declare*";—and then they pray the king and queen "that it may be *declared* and enacted that *all and singular* the rights and liberties *asserted and declared* are the true *ancient* and indubitable rights... *(The emphasis is Locke's.)*

The warning is simple. Revolutions should not throw out the baby with the bath water.

The Left largely believes citizens should be free but highly regulated to assure some ill-defined Progressive belief in the 'general will'. Robespierre believed that the French rebels should cleanse the government of its past and replaced by a *general will* assured by force. As previously mentioned, the path from the French Revolution runs through socialist history to today's American Left. The result is the 'general will' may not fully embrace the simple things that create greatness like work and family, faith and liberty.

Though the American Revolution broke with the English King and the English Empire, the Founding Fathers drew from the best English ideas to build our democracy. These ideas included property rights, rule of law and individual rights. As important, during the Constitutional Convention the Founding Fathers knew that over a century of sovereignty of the states had to be balanced with the rights of man and with some new structure for a central government that would balance the power of all. They did not throw the English nor Colonies' history away, but kept the baby and some of the bath water and invented a new style of government which had well-defined limits - federalism. And then, being somewhat unsure of this new beast it had created, added the Bill of Rights to assure our God-given rights could not be usurped by government and with a built in regulator of government's size, the Tenth Amendment which provides that all federal powers not granted in the Constitution are reserved for the states and the people. Trust, but verify.

Eighteenth century world leaders thought the American experiment in democracy was a bit crazy. As discussed earlier in *Deficiencies,* Europe's rural agricultural workers and early shopkeepers were considered not cut from the same cloth from which the Gentry were. To give these denizens the vote seemed outrageous, to be eligible for leadership undignified. Though the notion of the Left did not exist in during the 17th and 18th centuries, the pessimism of the Left is a logical extension of the arrogance of the Gentry. Those serfs and commoners outside the ruling class were considered not fully competent to lead their lives and needed the guiding and wise hand of the rulers whose wisdom was divined by God or by force. This arrogance is much in keeping with Leftist theory and policy today. The Founding Fathers rightly grappled with the notion of individual rights and with the inherent responsibilities coupled with liberty and ultimately decided that with great responsibilities should come great rights. They choose to raise up our citizenry by making them equal partners in creating this great republic. This optimism *is* the driving force for American greatness. Without this optimism as the foundation of our nation, Liberal democracy withers and dies. The American Liberal spirit is very powerful. Even with the increasingly heavy weight of a growing Leftist government over the last century, hard work, creativity and innovation, dragged along the government's dead weight and burdens, and still managed to produce both great wealth and a greater society. The weight of our government though is a burden that is not without cost and increasingly our society and its economy has slanted on a slow downward deflating or abilities and disengaging its citizens. The power of the citizenry is still written clearly in the Constitution.

That citizens were granted right to vote and the ability to be elected our nation's leaders coupled easily with a vote they had already enjoyed in colonial America, an economic vote. Milton Friedman stated that 'History suggests that capitalism is a necessary condition for political freedom.' A steady flowing river of Europeans came to America seeking only to work and work freely for their prosperity, drawn by the promise of free land to farm, land they could *own*, land by which they could earn their own keep. Being able to vote for their leaders was a continuing validation that their economic and political voice would be always heard. America's power of property and the vote changed the face of civilization.

Five centuries of the English of property ownership which had formerly focused on the nobility's ownership of property, transformed an entire continent where the common man could own property. Where only two centuries earlier, English land surveyor's major responsibilities were to inventory the Crown's assets throughout the Kingdom from noble's land to tenant farmers assets including livestock, American's surveyors legally specify the exact geography of property to assure legal ownership. Land surveyors cemented the legal right to land and assured that individual economic interests were an inherent American economic proposition. Land deeds were obtained and publically published to guarantee ownership and allowed property to become a leverageable asset that would create vast American wealth over the next two centuries. America was open for business both for agriculture and for the impending industrial boom. Unlike much of the world, Americans owned land – property. When Jefferson wrote the Declaration of Independence, he may have replaced Locke's notion of nature rights of 'life, liberty, and estate' (property) with 'life, liberty, and the pursuit of happiness' because Americans already had access to land. Americans had shocking economic freedom unknown in the world. And they had to right to vote to choose who would lay both the political and economic foundations for our country. Such a confluence of freedoms was unknown to man and a magnet for people around the world who wished to participate in the Great Experiment.

Though our current economic and political freedoms are in continuous decline, our ability to vote for political candidates as well as the products we purchase are still unparalleled. Trust and verify has evolved into a two-way process. Our political votes send winners to Washington and the same ability to vote can bring them home just as quickly. Economic freedom parallels this process. Where great economic power had been concentrated in large corporations, today, the vote of the consumer is now more than ever the arbiter of any business' success. The consumer is king, empowered by internet communications which provide nearly instant information about product quality via customer feedback. Bad products are quickly cycled out of the economy and better products quickly thrive. Bad companies either wither and pass to the netherworld or transform themselves and their products to win another day. More than ever, businesses take the pulse of their customers to understand if they are providing the quality solutions that they need.

Whereas businesses take customer satisfaction more and more seriously, government has completely missed the boat regarding measuring success or failure of government policy and focuses more on marketing and presenting a pretty face instead of producing a great product and well run government. A politician's success is based on whether he or she can raise a fabulously large campaign treasure chest, rent-seeking for dollars that ultimately support the status quo instead of needed change. Politicians believe the American voters are not paying attention and many are not as very good marketing can easily mask poor solutions with good marketing. But not trusting the voters with the difficult truths assure that politicians do not make difficult decisions. Like any company producing a bad product, at some point marketing campaigns fail to win over the customer's confidence and lack of product quality hits the bottom line. The American public understands something is amiss in Washington, but a glut of misinformation and glittering generalities obfuscate the real issues. When government ineffectiveness finally hits the fan with another financial crisis, a new trusted relationship will be much harder to build. The culture of avoidance has very high cost. Unfortunately these costs will be borne by our children. In effect our government avoids leadership because our children cannot vote yeah or nah on our slowly devolving economy or the huge debt our government is accruing. America has become the proverbial frog in the pot of water. The heat is on. Will the frog leap out before the water boils?

The culture of any organization, whether private or public, is driven from the top, from its leaders. Great leaders set out simple, measurable metrics for success, a vision of how to drive toward those metrics, and strategies and tactics for reaching those objectives. That vision for America, prior to our slide toward a Leftist Democracy focused on our individual political and economic liberties as the catalysts for greatness and the notion that a great society is built by us, the citizens, from the bottom up. This vision, the trust in individual greatness, has become a political plaything. When legislators begin to bargain and trade at the Congressional policy feast, this vision is lost, trampled by monopoly creation, rent-seeking, and burdensome regulation. Yet two centuries after building our original social contract, most every business in America understands that the success of their company is built by its people. Business leaders get the fact that without personal success, corporate success is very difficult at best. Why our political elite is moving away from the trust in its citizens to build a great society is more an indictment of the political parties than the individual legislators, but our politics are at odds with the original Liberal intent of the Constitution and today's modern organizational theory that that mimics it. Diverging from the wise Liberal mission of our founding fathers puts our nation on the slippery slope to reduced productivity, economic mediocrity and culture bifurcation.

The road back to great governance relies on leaders who are willing return to our traditional cultural pillars of governance which made America great; faith with reason, decentralized power, hard work and individual liberty. Optimism in individual liberty must be matched by visionary policy that relies on free citizens to build their own roads to success. Finding leaders that believe in Liberal Democracy will be the challenge of the 21st century.

Efficiency One: Liberal Economics: Free Markets and Capitalism

As there is no real world example of a perfect monopoly, there is also no example of perfectly free markets or capitalism. They don't exist. The struggle for precise definitions is muddled by reality and the reality is these ideas shadow one another's path, often combining in ways that can have both beneficial and detrimental effects. Markets seldom work freely and often require some basic superstructure provided by government. Even the capital in capitalism is improved by uniform rules for reserves required to cover loans and investments. At the opposite end of the economic spectrum, monopolies are seldom driven by simplicity or efficient enabling legislation.

The chief difference between the Liberal approach and Leftist is the spirit and intent of government to govern. Should regulation focus on maximizing choice for the individual? Should all markets be equally free? Does the making of bread require the same amount of regulation as banking and finance? Should clean water regulations have the same standards for energy companies and manufacturers? Should Nevada have to comply with very low arsenic standards with its already high content of groundwater arsenic, compared to Kansas that is already below the standard of 10 parts per billion?

The Left generally hopes to control, or own, the means of production. The Liberal attempts to find the minimal superstructure for a market to thrive and then distribution decision making as far toward the citizen as possible. Ultimately, though, these two perspectives of governance are not defined by two dots at the endpoints of a line, but are often a series of dots along a continuum. It does not take much movement along the line from Liberal to Left to feel the heavy weight and inefficiency of government and the decline of individual empowerment. Considering the citizen's arsenic issue, does the government need to do more than set a standard and let the cities and states determine what is reasonable for their locality. Well, according to the EPA, the City of Fallon, Nevada had levels of arsenic above the Federal Standard. High levels of leukemia are evident in the city, but no science links leukemia and arsenic. Is there a problem in Fallon? Yes, there is. Is it arsenic? Perhaps, perhaps not, as there are also high levels of jet fuel in the ground water and jet exhaust fumes in the air. (Klearman, 2007) The EPA compliance notification sucks the air out of the ability of local government and citizens to work with the military base and state officials to find the best solution. In this case, the Left in Washington aren't trying to control the means of production, but the means of regulation.

The points along the line from a free market to full government dominion are bracketed by both the need for government to set rules of civil and business interaction as well as a long history of political desire to derive power from centrally-managed markets. The desire for power feeds the need for centrally planned solutions that require more taxes. Few leaders political, business or even religious understand that great power is derived from extending power and responsibilities to their minions. Pope Francis may be the kind of leader we should all emulate. In an effort to rein in church The Guardian reported that to Pope said that 'The Roman Catholic Church, from the lowliest priest to the pontiff himself, must strip itself of all '"vanity, arrogance and pride" and humbly serve the poorest members of society.' (Pullella, 2013) Though the Pope may not be a capitalist or free marketer, his thoughts about leadership are both humble and inspiring. The first rule of Liberalism is to enable both the richest and the poorest with the tools to find every nook and cranny of personal greatness. Markets, all markets, allow the individual to earn success one small chunk at a time whether though economic exchange or the hard work to monetize personal value. As markets grow, personal value grows, society and culture matures - everyone is raised up.

Free markets are not a modern invention. This Liberal end of the economic spectrum sprung from medieval markets and bazaars where surplus goods were bartered for in a common area. Both people in this economic transaction had something to lose especially as an equal exchange of value was hard to assess for both parties. How many pounds of flour equaled the value of a pig? How many pounds of potatoes equaled a pair of shoes? No common value of exchange existed. The proliferation of money coined and valued by that state improved markets as transactional value became more transparent. As simple transactions in a market moved from common areas to shops and the very early retail environment, the notions about the quality of goods, even the quality of the business itself, its reputation, added a subjective dimension to the market.

Markets, today, are vast and diverse. Many are lightly regulated. Many more are heavily regulated with thousands of pages of regulations with which to comply. Large corporations employ hordes of legal staff and spend millions on software that assures compliance. Human relations departments have a litany of state, federal and union rules with which to comply. Public accounting has rules – lots and lots of rules. For publicly traded businesses, the very expensive rules of Sarbanes-Oxley preside. For privately owned businesses, accounts rules are a simpler set of accounting rules. Clean air rules. There are safety rules. Tax rules abound. The more heavily regulated the market, the higher the barrier to entry for establishing a business.

According to the federal government's Office of Management and Budget, regulations cost America, most $83.7 billion and benefited Americans nearly $800 billion. (Office of Management and Budget, 2012) The National Federation of Independent Business had a slightly different perspective they estimated the costs for regulatory compliance at $515 billion and that one of the top concerns for businesses where the government's regulatory reach and requirements. (Small Businesss for Sensible Regulations, 2013) Certainly the government is trying to protect is position that its regulation benefits Americans more than it costs, and the National Federation of Businesses is making a plea for a less weighty regulatory environment. Splitting the difference for the two numbers still equates to $300 billion is regulatory costs. What does it cost American's when an entrepreneur doesn't create a business or when a competitor decides to flee a market when regulations bog down the ability to compete?

According to the Centers for Disease Control there are only a handful of manufactures of flu vaccines. The government's highly restrictive environment for purchase of these vaccines drove all but a few from this business. Because there are so few manufacturers of flu vaccine, the government only orders a single strain of flu for the vaccine though many strains may be hitting the mainland. On the other hand, manufacturers of bread are lightly regulated and a plethora of vendors are ready for business every morning at 4 a.m. when the bakers arrive at work. Having only a few players in any industry because the government has regulated the competition away, is a clear sign that government has over-stepped it boundaries. Is there a specific red line where a market moves away from just the right' amount of regulation is a huge challenge. The first rule, seldom enjoined by government, is whether the economic impact is greater than the economic benefit. As the differing numbers from the NFIB and the OMB suggest above, the rules for measurement seem to be open to debate. What is a reasonably Liberal regulatory environment versus not-so-Liberal interventions is a hard assessment.

When Richard Nixon created the Environmental Protection Agency, it made sense both to set standards for clean air and water and also that industry would seek to assure that the regulations created were evenly implemented across an industry to assure open and fair competition – and get clean air and water, too. It is not surprising that business is often complicit in creating regulation to even the playing field and assure reasonableness. What should be surprising is how much money and time is spent by business lobbyists positioning regulation that would create advantage for their business over their competition. Sadly, extracting favors from government is a full time job for business lobbyists.

According to the Wall Street Journal, a 2011 IRS regulation 'all tax preparers would be forced to get a federal license.' (Wall Street Journal, 2013) Our hearts should be warmed to know that our government is protecting our tax interests. No one would want an unscrupulous tax-preparer. But was assuring the capabilities of a tax preparer the aim of government or business? Probably not. More from the Wall Street Article, 'A Charlotte, North Carolina owner of 22 Jackson Hewitt stores said that "more regulation is good us" because he had been "seeing a decline in the business because of all these moms and pops who open up out of nowhere."' God forbid, the Joe Tax Prepared armed with H&R Block Tax software would compete with, well, H&R Block for customers. Licensing is a bellweather for decreasing market competition.

Tax credits are the most easily identified. There are tax credits for solar and wind. In fact, there are a plethora of tax incentives for the energy industry. GE's 2010 consolidated financials show tax credits total $4.5 billion. It is no wonder they paid no taxes that they. On the other hand, Apple made over $40 billion in profits and paid $14 billion in taxes. Why does GE get tax preferences that Apple doesn't? Energy, though, is only the tip of the iceberg. There are employment incentives for hiring the poor, via Temporary Assistance Needy Families and the Work Opportunity Tax Credit for business. US News and World Reports published the top ten incentives for business. Among the many, there are business. There are incentives for accelerated depreciation. Deductions are allowed equal to a portion of taxable income attributable to domestic production. Expensing research and experimentation. Exclusion of interest on hospital construction bonds, and on life insurance interest. A credit for low-income housing investments. (Moeller, 2013) And these are just from the top ten. There are hundreds of tax incentives, perhaps thousands. Most if not all of the incentives is because business had their hand out for special dispensations. They don't mind paying their indulgences but would like a discount. But business isn't the only culprit. The government has been both a market maker and a market killer.

The EPA's 2013 463 page, 'Standards of Performance for Greenhouse Gas Emissions from New Stationary Sources: Electric Utility Generating Units,' is a great example of the government's attempt to control a market. (EPA, 2013) Richard Nixon and

Congress collaborated to create the EPA in 1970 with the mission to help set a reasonable economic playing field polluting industries to have a standard set of goals for clean air and water. There was certainly nothing in the enabling legislation that would encourage the EPA to expand its role to include the management of CO2 as a dangerous material or per the 'Standards of Performance' set out to attack a specific method of producing energy, in this case rendering the coal market economically enviable. The EPA's 'Standards' missile coerces markets, reduces both market and personal choices, and harms the economy in general.   This executive intrusion into Congressional affairs can also be seen in the FCCs attempt to initiate Net Neutrality by fiat or the Justice Department's challenge to Louisiana's Voucher system that helps poor children obtain a private school education.   Are these intrusions really meant to enable and enrich our personal lives or some errant notion of the 'General Will' as perceived by bureaucrats? Ask the kid in Louisiana who may lose his voucher to go to a private school.

Although many citizens would consider the government's intrusion into General Motor's bankruptcy in 2009 an inappropriate intrusion in the markets, and it is, a less well-known intrusion is the EPA's CAFE (Corporate Average Fuel Economy) standards which have gone through several renditions since the first iteration in 1975 after the Arab Oil Embargo. New standards adopted this year will push a typical sedan's fuel economy from today's 36 to 61 miles per gallon in 2025. The central planning assumes that a technology will exist to produce such a vehicle. This standard presumes that gasoline will be the fuel of choice in 10 years. How much additional investment will be spent on improving gas fuel economy over the next decade instead of for innovations that may have nothing at all to do with gasoline engines is unclear? Regardless, the basis for this kind of government standard setting isn't to improve our lives but to market the notion that the government is doing something useful.   Instead of micromanaging the gasoline engine, the government might set broad goals for energy independence or creating simpler and sensible financial regulation would produce far more benefit than Congressional endeavors for CAFE.

What would reasonable market approaches be for energy or finance. Energy may be the easiest. A prolific commodity market needs only an open market. No one energy resource will solve our problems, but the significant intrusion of government into energy has mucked up the efficiencies of delivering energy to its customers. Removing tax incentives from every segment – oil, nuclear, solar, electric car incentives, everything, would allow the markets to generate the cleanest, most efficient energy sources and allow capital to flow to new technologies that will change the landscape of the market. Doing so would accelerate the personalization of energy which should occur about mid-century with consumer products available to plug into the grid and generate power for personal use as well as power for grid consumption. Every single tax credit and tax incentive moves dollars away from replacement energy sources to alternative energy sources like the economically costly solar panels or hybrid cars. Tax perversions like these are Leftist notions based on belief and desire that markets can be planned and controlled to the benefit of the General Will. In reality, their ingenuity increases costs and slows innovation.

In the financial sector, over-regulation and central planning has increased costs to consumers and created bubbles in the mortgage and equities markets. For equities, Quantitative Easing has added liquidity to the economy to the tune of $85 billion per month for three years. This is equivalent to about 6% of GDP. The economy is growing at 2% a year. The difference 4% is the additional money in the economy that needs to go somewhere. Most of these additional dollars have created a bubble in equities and the home buyer's market, driving both markets to not-so-reasonable valuation. In equities, the stock market is up 33% in two years, whereas the economy has grown only 4%. Reading the tea leaves, this means that the companies included in the DOW Jones average reallllllllly did well and the rest of the economy really did badly, or, there the market is overvalued because the extra dollars from the Fed are seeking the best return. Since there are very few companies experiencing double digit growth, the real reading of the tea leaves is that there is a bubble. Is central planning helping or simply prolonging an economic resizing the economy desperately needs.

Banking is another great example of central planning gone wrong.

As conservative as many retail banks are in conducting their business, investment banks tend toward greed. Where retail bank transaction are measured in thousands or millions, investment banks risk billions and tens of billions. When sensible regulations for vetting a mortgage loan candidate are tossed to the wind, which is what happened during the run up to the 2008 financial meltdown, lenders race to make money where there was little to none to be made before. Greed wins where the loot seems to be free. That individual mortgages could be packaged as mortgage backed securities, small loans by banks became very large and tradable commodities, traded by very large institutions as well as small. Couple all this with what looked like a reasonable path to deregulation of the industry with the 1999 end of Glass-Steagall from the FDR administration which broke up commercial and investment banking and well, stir in nearly free money from the Fed, and an economic bubble formed and exploded.

The response from our government was not take a very serious look at the challenge created by an oligopoly of just a few very large banks versus a more competitive environment of many smaller banks – a return to something like Glass-Stegeall. Dodd-Frank simply propped up banks that were Too Big To Fail with guarantees of government protection should failure occur. Additionally, the also Too Big To Fail Freddie Mac and Fannie Mae come out of the 2009 Financial Crunch unscathed. As they assumed the risk for hundreds of billions in bad loans the government instead of pushing them to End of Life status doubled down and bought their bad debt. These are not actions of a Liberal government but a Leftist government intent on expanding its network of corporate friends, which is the next step in government intrusion.

Crony capitalism is just short of the path along the continuum to Corporatism or state capitalism. What deals were made in the back rooms in the halls of our Federal government while discussing the bail out of the major banks in 2008-9 is not fully known. The outcome though is certain. These banks now have special consideration as a special collective of very large banks. The special dispensation is that their cost of money from the Fed is less than that provided to smaller banks and community banks largely because of the protections of big banks and reduced risk associated with Dodd-Frank. Should the economy go bump in the night, the Fed has funding to protect against bank failure that small banks do not. So not only did the government miss the mortgage bubble which it created, not only did the government coerce JP Morgan to purchase Bear Stearns in hopes to escaping the results of the mortgage debacle, but when all was said and done, the government guaranteed near perpetual existence to several large banks regardless of their conduct or the government's incompetence. How do legislators so completely miss solving the problems of the financial crisis and opt instead.

The step from cronyism to corporatism is not a great step and certainly the deals our government made with GM, Chrysler, the major banks, and the major Pharmaceutical and Insurance companies (Obamacare). Corporatism is the dandy step that Mussolini took in Italy, reining in the power of businesses under the umbrella of the government's General Will. In Fascism, the umbrella of protection is coerced physically with force. The business leader is either 'with us or against us,' and if against use the options may not be pleasant. In the less Fascist approach, Corporatism is the coercion that is less formidable than a quick trip to a jail cell without a trial, but the end result may not be different as political greed has large tender values to exchange of political goods. Being on the wrong side of a government too willing to exercise its power is generally not a good thing.

Communistic Capitalism as practiced in China is a vast array of market implementations across the spectrum which literally include community bazaars, street vendors, free trade zones and government owned businesses and banks, and a highly centrally-planned economy. If governments should experiment to discover more paths to prosperity, then China is at the top of the list. One test not included in this long list is whether Friedman was correct that capitalism is a necessary condition for freedom. Short of a new constitution and bill or rights democracy may not arrive in China without revolution. But the Chinese success, largely built on massive amounts of private investment flowing into China following a society rich with low paid and well-educated laborers, is a constant Siren's song for America's left. Both countries are embroiled in economic controversy surrounding the production and export of solar panels. This is a duel of crony capitalists. John Smirnow, vice president for competitiveness for SEIA (Solar Energy Industry Association) had this to say about a recent deal between the countries regarding 'dumping' of underpriced solar panel from China to countries around the world.

> 'The problem we have right now is that the trading
> rules are not working well. Solar has a very complex
> global supply chain' and 'relying on the existing system
> to settle trade disputes isn't working. (Wingfield, 2013)

There should be little wonder that both sides are befuddled as both governments made private investments in solar manufacturing firms for which both countries have paid dearly in significant losses. The American government has further complicated the situation by adding residential and utility subsidies for purchasing solar panels. If Mr. Smirow sounds a bit like the whiny James Taggart in Atlas Shrugged looking to government to assure the success of an industry, well, he does. His mission is to assure the US artificially pumps up the American market to buy solar panels as much as is unreasonably possible. The further these two governments insert themselves into the market, the more complex and expensive the solutions will be.

The final step along the Liberal/Left line is scientific socialism, communism – full government control of the means of production and ownership of property. In the Communist ladder to social perfection, the Dictatorship of the Proletariat, a precursor to social nirvana which is never reached. One man, one vote, once! Like every government, aging and maturity all too often translates into the politics or power of self-protection of that power. Once all powerful, the status quo predominates. The final step on the ladder of Communism is never reached because the Prols never meet the standards required by communism; never seem to learn what it takes to be perfect.   In Marx's rendition of perfect, the final state of communism, the state at which the 'general will' resonates with perfect economic harmony and near perfect allocation of resources sounds much like capitalism, laissez faire economics and a full democracy absent the republic.   But again, perfection tends not to find earthly haunts.

Understanding the many of the elements of this continuum from markets to monopoly, from capitalism to socialism is important as a guide to identify how these elements which were seldom part of American governance for two centuries *are now regular fare in the government's daily activities.*   Citizens should find power grabs by government for erecting monopolies an inappropriate design of any policy. Voters should understand that government by presidential fiat (e.g. the exclusion of House Staff from Obamacare or EPA's decision by fiat, without Congressional Approval, to regulate CO2 - EPA is part of the executive branch) is a breach of faith with the people and the Constitution. No Liberal should find the government purchase of companies (GM and Chrysler) or investment in companies (Solyndra) unacceptable governance.   These types of governance move America down a path to the Deficiencies of Leftist Democracy, and if Marx is correct, and then to a revolution of the masses followed by the Dictatorship of the Proletariat.

As Friedman was quoted earlier, 'history suggests that capitalism is a necessary condition for political freedom.'   The freedom to buy bread where you want, the type of bread you want, at a price that is agreeable is just another type of vote. When the government deprives you of any of your potential choices, it deprives you of your vote. Although the notion that 'Capitalism is the worst economic system except for all the others,' was actually a slightly different a quote by Winston Churchill about Democracy: 'It has been said that democracy is the worst form of government, except all those others that have been tried.' Perhaps misquoting the maxim is simply a Freudian slip. Rightly, both quotes work well together, as they have here in America since its beginnings. In both capitalism and democracy lay the essential quality for building a great society and dominating economy: that the individual at the center of their philosophies and the building block for personal, corporate and national success. The individual is the kernel upon which civil and economic society is built.

So why does a free market economy succeed better than an economy that falls along the Leftish Continuum of government intervention? Is it as simple as the fact the 300,000,000 million people making sound economic decisions daily to purchase a product or service from tens of millions of businesses that are selling the products is more efficient that 537 elected federal officials and a few thousand states officials trying to structure our daily economic decisions. That the government could do more than set a basic structure for our economic affairs seems intellectually impossible. Our well-oiled, free-markets are the extension of the exercise of our personal freedoms. The individual is why markets achieve efficiency where monopolies seldom if ever do? Our decisions are fast and innovation faster. Government is slow and plodding and completely unable to match the flexibility and velocity of markets. Why does central planning and government monopolies and crony capitalism deliver such poor results and free markets do? It's in the numbers.

When 300,000,000 people make economic decisions, price decisions, product decisions every day the best set of products at the best prices win. Losers change or go out of business. In a very competitive environment, which free markets should necessarily be very competitive, new entrants change the market landscape or potentially end one market by creating a new one via Schumpeter's notion of creative destruction.

The second to second dynamic of a market is that efficiency in price and effectiveness in the quality and diversity of products is maximized. Whereas my neighbor may wish to purchase a Lexis for $79,000, another neighbor may wish to buy a Honda Civic for $20,000 and both get high quality. A third person may find a $2,000 '97 Camry the best buy. The clearance section at Walmart has bread for 99 cents or less, but the high-end AJ's market a mile away has fresh Ciabatta for $4.00. And there are whole sections of different types and styles of breads at each market. The poor person can afford bread as easily as the rich person. Markets are broad and diverse. Monopolies are skinny and constricted. With Capitalism and markets, change is constant; improvement is constant; flexibility is constant because the voter determines what is needed. As a nation adopts Leftist positions, central planning reduces the flexibility of the marketplace, extinguishes change, and kills innovation.

Democracy should work in parallel to the flexibility of markets. When politicians fail to meet the needs of the people, new politicians arrive to replace the old. As the political parties are being held in very low esteem, will a 'political market' innovation change the parties or create a new perhaps. Perhaps. In a less regulated market (think McCain-Feingold which assure near locks for a vast majority of our Congressional districts) parties would proliferate. Our issue today is there are no new products to purchase in the political marketplace. No creative destruction has occurred. The Tea Party made a slight bump in the political continuum, but nothing has replaced the status quo because so much money is spent to protect the Federal Golden Goose. Will the political market be induced to change? Perhaps so.

Understanding the efficiency of markets compared to monopolies is an easy intellectual exercise. The 'Just Right' of government regulation of markets is less clear. Government must be a referee, not a player in markets. Primary objectives of Liberal governance assure that power remain distributed and that the individual be the focus of economic activity. To that end, some guiding principles may make sense:

- Does the regulation level the playing field for competitive engagement or minimize competition?

- Does the regulation assure maximum choices for the buyer of product or services?
- Does the regulation place the government as the creative destroyer or the innovator or investor of innovators?
- Does the regulation make the citizen less responsible for economic decisions?
- Does the federal government assure that power for decisions does not enrich the position of the federal government?

Where does wise regulation end and unreasonable regulation start? What is Just Right? Hayek sheds a bit of light: 'To prohibit the use of certain poisonous substances, or to require special precautions in their use, to limit working hours or to require certain sanitary arrangements, is fully compatible with the preservation of competition. The only question here is whether in the particular instance the advantages gained are greater than the social costs which they impose.' (Hayek, 1944)

Measuring the 'advantages gained' versus social costs is a major challenge when the amount of political power to be gained or lost is at stake. Though it is becoming more and more clear how the government's social monopolies are clearly both financially costly but also socially and culturally expenses, political market creates significant fear, uncertainty and doubt in the citizenry. Rolling granny over the cliff as the possible outcome for Paul Ryan's restricting of Medicare was great and effective theatre by the Left. Similar messages are delivered when any changes to the Left's power is challenged in education, welfare, water and air regulations, actually anything with a budget line item except perhaps the military.

There may be one metric that even the most average of citizens might be able to gauge whether the effects of free markets will be degraded or the regulation that is needed is stepping from reasonable to onerous. If the legislation takes more than 50 pages to articulate a remedy to the supposed problem the perhaps the legislators should start over as they probably don't understand either the markets or the problem they are solving well enough to create a good solution.

JUST RIGHT

Efficiency Two: Command, Manage and Enable

The Command and Control structure of the federal executive branch (military, health, education, EPA, SEC, and a host of others) has been built to assure Americans' daily activities measure up <u>to the needs of the government!</u>   Not unlike military organizations during the time of war, the different layers of government gives a command and everyone follows orders.   The military, though, has a daily mission very different from yours or mine, which includes life and death, and so control is essential to its mission.

In our daily lives, we do not need a dictator, general, or president to order our daily activities, and wisely, most of us would and do resent such an environment.   America's social monopolies mimic the military as they attempt to constrain our activities and the various markets to bend them to the government's will.   Like the military, these market constraints and ordering of personal activities are very expensive to create and control.   Adding complexity to the control equation exacerbates execution.

Regulatory Command (with Less Control and More Management)

The alternative to command and control is command and manage or command and organize.   Great government results from providing a modest super-structure for all of us to compete fairly for resources and for wise entrepreneurs to create new resources when current solutions are poor or scarce.

As Leftist governance presumes that those who need to be regulated are too focused on their own needs and cannot possibly understand the public good as well as government can, Liberal governance assumes that its citizens will generally act in reasonable ways that produce reasonable outcomes.   In a recent Science Daily Article, Dirk Helbing and Thomas Grund, discovered what they thought to be new social patterns that might breed new economic theory. Their theory is a restatement of ideas that are millennia old. Only the names are changed.

> While the "homo economicus" optimizes its utility independently, the "homo socialis" puts himself or herself into the shoes of others to consider their interests as well," explains Grund, and Helbing adds: "This establishes something like "networked minds". Everyone's decisions depend on the preferences of others." This becomes even more important in our networked world. (Grund, 2013)

Grund and Helbing may believe their notion of homo socialis is something new, but the notion that we put ourselves in someone else's shows is as old as 'Do onto to others as you would have them do unto you.' Even Adam Smith theorized an invisible hand that guides over economic transactions, the result of which produces efficiencies in the market. This hand belongs to homo socialis.

The important assumption by the Left is that we are all Homo Economicus. In reality, excepting for a few, we are all Homo Socialis. We self-organize. We understand when exchanges of goods are not reasonable. We park inside the lines at the shopping center. Occasionally, Economicus erupts from our personalities, but common self provides boundaries. In government, when Homo Economicus or Homo Regulatus, the onerous regulators, get too much power, homo socialis is kicked to the side of the road. This is a pattern that parallels the growth of power in government.

For Liberalism to rise to its zenith in the regulator environment, the Liberal regulator's presumptions about government must start with the need for freedom to of individuals to make social and economic decisions without government assistance. Homo Economicus will always need to be regulated, but not to the point where we are all harmed.

If the cultural pillars of good governance of faith with reason, decentralization, hard work and liberty, then what the tools for Liberal legislators should use to design the legal foundation upon which we compete for resources? They are:

- Trust (and Verify)
- Simplicity
- Transparency
- Curiosity

Is this list too short? Perhaps, but obeying the second tool of this short list, the rule of simplicity, brevity is a faster route to wisdom than complexity, so four tools should suffice.

Trust

Trust is a primary element of great leadership, but trust is also a pivotal tool for Liberal governance. When erecting legal foundations for non-criminal law, without trust in the people in their political, religious, social and economic habits, then simplicity is not possible, and transparency not needed, as the resulting government will produce cranky edifices like Obamacare that micro-manage and control citizen habits.

Trust is a team sport. In basketball, great leadership is demonstrated by great point guards. There are those that distribute the ball to the open player and shoot only when needed and maximizes the effect of everyone on the floor. Trust builds the abilities of team mates. Less trusting point guards tend to make their own shots and use the other players as a last resort. Steve Nash is a great leader, displaying trust in his players and enriching the power and capabilities of each teammate on the court. Allen Iverson on the other hand, a life-long high performer who shot first and passed on occasion, was not much of a distributor. He might have been better suited as a shooting guard. Steve made his team better. Allen made his stats better. Great leaders make their team better and do not seek accolades or power.

Trust begins with a pass, as does verification of that trust. The pass is a delegation of power. Trust is validated with a high percentage of made baskets and low turnover rates. If not, the coach will change the lineup perhaps with guidance from Mr. Nash. Without the pass, Allen is a one-man show, a situation that makes winning hard.

Legislation should create trust through the dispersion of power, based on a simple fact that markets do indeed work, that the citizen is indeed wise and responsible. Though there are selfishly interested citizens, the self-interest of the masses assures equal exchange of value in transactions and continually seeks this exchange to build lasting economic, social and cultural relationships. Without trust in the American people, a legislative tyranny evolves as it has over the last 100 years, building onerous regulation and a never-ending succession of economic and social monopolies.

Transparency

Transparency is the *essential* tool for building lasting economic, political and social resilience. Transparency makes relationships durable. Transparency is public and visible. Transparency is the antidote for greed, and fraud, and the lawless. Transparency is a magnet for all those citizens around the world seeking a home for their business because America is a haven for transparency.

The lack of transparency of mortgage-backed securities led to the 2008 market crash. Lots of blame was laid at the feet of greedy banks and mortgage lenders, but the cascade of problems created by easy credit, no-docs or stated income loans (new solutions erected by the government i.e. trust without verification) made it easier for poorer Americans to get a loan, which led to a storm of bad loans packaged inside completely non-transparent mortgage-backed securities. Loans, regardless of quality were packaged by the thousands, into mortgage-backed securities and rated AAA without so much of a hint at the actual quality of the individual loans. As mortgage loans had always been of good quality (because lending standards had always been high) rating agencies looked no further than *Mortgage* in mortgage-back securities to decide the quality of the investment. Again, the quality of the loans were hidden for the buyers.

The superiority of American economics is tremendously high because economic transactions have always been pristine and visible. Stocks are only as good as audited financials. Mutual Funds are rated, based on the quality of each stock in its portfolio. Closer to home, the price of bread labeled in the market, is the price, unless it is on sale, then the sale price is the price. Our land investments are based on the Title to the land and the well-articulated geographic position of the land, and a long and visible paper trail to assure that Title is free and clear before purchase. Our savings are safe in banks because we know banks must keep a certain amount of our money in reserve. Contracts for transactions are published, signed and uniformly available. Immigrant business people come to the US because it is one of the few places on earth where transparency is so high. It is the expectation not the exception. Transparency creates a land of plenty where haggling is generally not required, not for the buyer to get the lowest price so he can feed his family, nor for the seller, so he can feed his. America business is business because it is one of the few countries in the world where riches are almost uniformly created by hard work not fraud and corruption.

Our mutual trust is propelled to greater heights because transparency is a crucial piece of trust and verification. Though corruption and greed are possible, both in our commercial interests and in government, these are diminished because it is generally easy to spot corruption in a vast sea of open information. Trust is built when Homo Economicus steps into the light. When Economicus goes too far, breeches the law, Americas very independent courts and judges are seldom enticed to corruption and adjudicate fairly and wisely.

Simplicity

If it is possible to build trust and transparency with very complex solutions, it is at best unlikely. Simplicity is essential to great problem-solving.

Simplicity. "The Dog and the Frisbee." The paper, presented by Andrew G. Haldane, Executive Director for Financial Stability at the Bank of England and co-authored by Vasileios Madouros.

> 'The paper notes that the Glass-Stegall Act, with its simple prohibitions on mixing commercial banking with investment banking, lasted sixty years, compared with just six for the complex rules of Basel II. It cites statistical evidence that in the period leading up to and during the recent financial crisis, simple indicators of bank soundness were better predictors of failure than complex ones.' (Dolan, 2012)

Siegel and Etzkorn took aim at our daily challenges in an increasingly complex society quoting Henry David Thoreau who died 150 years ago, 'simplicity, simplicity, simplicity.' Living at Walden was a superb diversion for Thoreau at alternative to life in what he considered the highly complex society of the late 1700s. Today's complexity is not so much broader as it is deeper and varied. We are confronted a wonderful litany of choices commercially, duplicated by a flush of diversity to transact business. Government, though, is making our lives and the lives of businessmen more complex and difficult with a very rapid rise for federal rules and regulations.

Credit card contracts have grown from a mere 400 words in 1980 to 20,000 words today. Our tax code once simple and short has grown to a Leviathan of over 1,000,000 words, longer than the Bible. Medicare's enabling legislation in 1967 took barely 140 pages. Time has served Medicare poorly as continual additions and fixes now run into thousands of pages. One can only imagine what Obamacare's incomprehensible 2000-page beginning will beget and which now stretches to over ten thousand pages. Both time and an unwillingness to bit off the hard work of finding creative and simple solutions allow complexity to thrive. Siegle and Etzkorn explain:

> 'How did we get into this mess? Lawyers and technologists are the taproots of complexity. Government regulators make things worse with misguided attempts to require "disclosure." Predatory companies with business practices that are onerous for consumers are only too happy to hide behind the cloak of complexity. And virtually all companies and organizations are averse to change and naturally inclined to take the path of least resistance.' (Etzkorn, 2013)

They add:

> 'Complexity is the coward's way out. But there is nothing simple about simplicity, and achieving it requires following three major principles: empathizing (by perceiving others' needs and expectations), distilling (by reducing to its essence the substance of one's offer) and clarifying (by making the offering easier to understand or use).' (Etxkorn, 2013)

Stanford's Design Thinking Institute parallels these thoughts. The curriculum teaches problem solving in a much different way than a lawyer. 'Students start in the field, where they develop empathy for people they design for, uncovering real human needs solutions, and create rough prototypes to take back out into the field and test with real people.' (Standford Design Thinking College, 2013)

Perhaps Homo Socialis, and empathy toward one another, is not just an intellectualism of professors but something common among American citizens.

Curiosity

More than empathy, distillation and clarifying are required. The students at Stanford, Siegel and Etzkorn, a vast horde of scientists and engineers, a few business leaders and a smattering of common folks strewn around America who ponder our mess in Washington, have one additional variable that is crucial for successful problem-solving, curiosity. For the curious, any ol' answer isn't good enough. Sometimes great solutions take a lifetime of work and tinkering to find a simple solution that works. The curious will not accept a complex solution. The curious will always dig deeper, seeking a unifying principle. The curious would not accept 10000 pages of tax regulation as a clean, effective solution for taxation. The curious seek simplicity as central criteria for a great solution.

As noted in Deficiencies, Einstein gave great direction for problem-solving: 'If you cannot explain it simply, you do not understand it well enough.' Not enough weight can ever be given to the notion of simplicity whether it regards the rules we make for our children, a sales process (Keep It Simple Stupid), The General Theory of Relativity ($E-MC^2$), or regulatory legislation, where sadly simplicity does not exist. When simplicity exits, a solution's effectiveness diminishes, sometimes to zero.

Efficiency Three: Example Market Solution: Healthcare and Retirement

If the history of monopolies is any guide, simplifying, deregulating, and de-monopolizing healthcare will with absolute assurance reduce the cost of services, improve innovation and correct our less than effective relationships with providers and physicians. The transition will look not unlike the breakup of AT&T. Some initial angst will quickly follow with a realization that prices are falling and options are increasing, rapidly, very rapidly.

The Left's, however, starts with a culture of centralization, of the need to care for citizens, to provide services at little or no costs, which leads to solutions for expanding government provided healthcare has founded on four premises about the nature of the problem:

- that many of us are unable to earn enough money to afford healthcare,
- that resources should be allocated to any and all persons equally,
- that government mandates to participate are required for equal access to healthcare, notably Obamacare, Medicaid and Medicare, and
- that an HMO/PPO solution provides the most effective, cost efficient care.

Put another way, for and effective and fair solution, government control is needed to redistribute dollars or chits, for insurance products that were very similar in coverage, to groups that were poor, aged or without insurance, with a financing tool that was both costly to the individual and beneficial for insurance companies revenue streams.

Poor government problem-solving always starts with solving the wrong problem. The Left, by taking a pessimistic attitude of the capabilities of Americans, by believing that a one size fits all product is efficient and effective, and mandates from government will provide uniform access and quality, completely missed the opportunities of free markets to provide solutions that result in quality solutions at the lowest cost.

Prior to interventions by the government, most patients paid cash services, but as technology improved and new innovations became available, insurance for hospitalization arrived and was generally inexpensive. In the '60s before Medicare and Medicaid were signed into law few Americans were unable to afford health insurance. But early market solutions were injured by government intervention with the advent of Nixon's HMO/PPO solution, federal monopolies Medicaid and Medicare, and now federal mandates for insurance for everyone via Obamacare.

Obamacare is the harshest government intervention, forcing everyone to buy government insurance whether they can afford it or not. This template for government interference is not a solution many of us are going to like, whether in healthcare or in any marketplace. Were the government to mandate ownership of a cell phone, Americans would be outraged. Being told what to use, what to buy or how to act, flies in the faces of American's love of liberty.

To understand how employing a market-based solution will reduce our individual health care costs, identifying all the costs that make up our total healthcare bill is crucial. They are the:

The Liberal's notion of expanding access to healthcare should be founded on four premises:

- that almost every citizens is able to earn enough money to afford healthcare,
- that having many options for financing health care is optimal,
- that government mandates to assure free access to healthcare from any provider is essential to an efficient health care market, and
- patients are the wisest arbiter of purchasing services at the best price (not government or an insurance company)

To understand how government monopolies and HMO/PPO mandates have increased the cost of the typical insurance policy, the following section lays out the costs and the expected benefits to moving to a free market solution. The dollar costs that are quoted are estimates, and should be seen as estimates for think tanks with greater resources than mine to haggle and debate. Regardless, a very large percentage of the average private insurance policy is not associated with the services acquired by the policy holder. Approximately 40% of the private bill is paid for services not rendered and equivalent to the inefficiencies caused by the intrusion of government health monopolies. Four costs associated with government intrusion:

- cost-shifting due to low payments from government programs to providers
- cost shifting for those with poor health behavior to those with good health behavior
- taxes paid in by workers for Medicare that go to someone retired, not the payer
- taxes paid for Medicaid that go to someone, but not the payer
- the high cost of government mandated HMO/PPO solutions and lack of flexibility of optional financing options (i.e. over-regulation of the insurance market)

Cost Shifting

Government has only two tools to curb costs: price fixing in the form of fee for benefit reductions and exclusion of benefits – not covering specific procedures or drugs. The government generally pays less for certain benefits, less than the market demand, so provider losses due to diminished government health care payments are transferred to the backs of health providers who then transfer some of this burden to the privately insured and cash payers. This shifting is not unlike AT&T's monopoly in which the loss in the residential phone market was shifted to the more profitable long distance market. The principle is the same for health care. Cost shifting due to low fee for service programs (Medicare, Medicaid and now Obamacare) increase private costs from 2% to 10%, depending on the source cited. Per Merrill Matthews And Mark E. Litow:

'However, Medicaid underpays hospitals for care, about 66% on average of what private health insurance would pay, according to the Centers for Medicare and Medicaid Services' (CMS) Office of the Actuary. And that percentage will decline.' (Litow, 2013)

As more cost shifting will occur with the expansion of Medicaid under Obama, with the entrance of Obamacare in 2014, and the doubling of Medicare recipients over the next 20 years, these shifts will triple. (For the purposes of the cost comparisons below, 15% will be used as the value for cost shifting. This is not an attempt to be exact. It is simply a conservative guess as costing shift will further impact the cost of private insurance.

Health Behavior

Second, our insurance is not rated for good health habits which shift health costs from those with poor health behavior to the healthy. Smokers pay the same rate as non-smokers. The obese pay the same rate the fit. For car insurance, those with bad habits like speeding or who have high accident rates pay higher rates. The same should be true for health insurance.

Not much could be simpler than the proposition that better health behavior leads to better health, so incentives for better behavior would be beneficial. The Left, however, has not seen the light on this optimistic note. During the Obamacare hearing during 2009, with great evidence at hand, in lock step the Democrats moved down the road of government dominance instead of personal responsibility. Steve Hurd, CEO of Safeway, during his Congressional testimony during the Obamacare hearing, noted that several behavioral factors were in play regarding poor health.

Mr. Hurd said this:

'Safeway's plan capitalizes on two key insights gained in 2005. The first is that 70% of all health-care costs are the direct result of behavior. The second insight, which is well understood by the providers of health care, is that 74% of all costs are confined to four chronic conditions (cardiovascular disease, cancer, diabetes and obesity). Furthermore, 80% of cardiovascular disease and diabetes is preventable, 60% of cancers are preventable, and more than 90% of obesity is preventable.' (Hurd, 2009)

By charging higher rates for workers with poor behaviors – poor diet, drinking, smoking and no exercise, and less for workers with good behavior, Safeway flattened their health care costs over four years.   When workers were responsible for their health, and higher cost resulted from poor behavior, employees changed their behavior. They changed their behavior and got healthier. This should be a 'duh' moment for just about anyone, but Left's religious fervor for a Single-Payer government solution, ignored health reality and the notion of personal responsibility in the form of a more responsible rating system.   Mr. Hurd's ideas were summarily ignored during the Obamacare deliberations.

Costly HMO/PPO

Third, the HMO/PPO solution is high cost to everyone. Clark Havighurst of Duke analyzed how the HMO-style insurance debilitates the health market.   "The market failure most responsible for economic inefficiency in the health-care sector is not consumers; ignorance about the quality of care, but rather their ignorance of the cost of care, which ensures that neither the choices they make in the marketplace nor the opinions they express in the political process reveal their true preferences.' (Havighurst, 2002)

Put another way, via the Adam Smith, there is no exchange of value between the purchaser and seller because the middleman (government or insurance companies) hide the actual cost. Add to Havighurst's concern the fact that the mandated financial tool of choice is the most expensive solution for payments: the HMO/PPO.

'The irony is that majoritarian politics, combined with the public's general unawareness of health care costs, allows the elite classes, including many self-proclaimed consumer representatives as well as organized professional groups, to design and maintain a system that meets their own particular needs but leaves less privileged citizens who are not qualified for publicly financed care with a Hobson's choice: either coverage for "Cadillac" care or no health coverage at all. Ruled as it is by and for dominant elites, the U.S. health care system imposes large, unfair, and unnecessary economic burdens on ordinary working people.' (Havighurst, 2002, p. 32)

The HMO/PPO treats every health issue as an insurable incident. Were Americans to purchase car insurance in the same manner, car washes, oil changes, tire repair and replacement and a host of other costs would be insurance events. The cost of car insurance would be astronomical and unaffordable for all but the wealthy few. So why mandate the most costly form of insurance? Well, insurance companies love it. Reallllly love it. If they only provided insurance for the costly events, premiums would drop by two-thirds, as would the value of their companies. Consider is type of regulated tariff a demi-monopoly, but a monopoly nevertheless.

Paying For Someone Else's Health

The final costs are taxes we pay but for which we receive no benefit. Today, these include Medicaid and Medicare. Obamacare will add several tax burdens. This program's burden will fall to taxes on the rich initially, and then on non-compliant businesses or individuals who accept the fine instead of choosing Obama's insurance plan, and finally on all of us. The poor and the young, though, will carry this burden when it hits the economy in 2014. For the average taxpayer the costs of Obamacare is not easily calculated and will not likely show up in his or her paycheck.

Medicare taxes are simple and direct. From everyone's paycheck 1.45% of total pay is deducted. America's median income is $44,000. Doing the math, the Average Joe and his family pay $53.15 a month. These taxes are not saved for Joe, but put in a pool of money deducted from American's checks and passed immediately on to someone who is retired. There is no future guarantee of benefits provided by the government that says the current taxpayer will get like benefits or any benefits when they retire because they have paid taxes.

For Medicaid the math is a bit different. There is not Medicaid tax as its funds are part of the general fund of which part is generated by the Federal Income tax. Because the taxes we pay are progressive, the rich pay much and many Americans pay no federal taxes at all. To arrive at an estimate of those who do pay taxes but are not rich, the math is a bit more complicated. Outlays for Medicaid totaled $278 Billion in 2011. There were approximately 135 million taxpayers, about half of which paid little or no taxes. Tax payers with high marginal tax rates, the rich (about 5% of the taxpayer base), paid 37.4%, leaving about 45% of taxpayers (us regular folks) to pay 62.4% of the $278 Billion of Medicaid outlays. As only about one quarter of all taxes collected is income taxes, the final bill to us regular folks is about $117.88 per month. Because the government borrows almost one third of the budget to pay its bills the math gets very blurry, but this discussion will be sidelined as borrowing has already been discussed as a liability.

For the average guy, these are very meaningful costs ($200 before taxes) each month for which no utility is gained. Imagine if one's family insurance were $200 less expensive each month. What would insurance for the average person cost were he not paying for the government's health monopolies, for someone else's poor health behavior, for a very expensive HMO/PPO. Much less. Very much less.

Pay Our Own Way Is Less Expensive

Can we simply terminate government monopolies and business provided medical benefits and transform healthcare insurance to market-based solutions? What would result? Change is always a bit scary. The unknown always is. Reality is far different. In a market where the Cadillac HMO/PPO were only one of a complete menu of options, millions of American's would drop insurance like a hot potato. Deregulating the one size all fits market to allow for more options focused primarily on tools for financing major health expenses like hospitalization and cancer regimens would dramatically reduce cost for policies.

Ending business-provided health benefits, though this would alarm the 150 million Americans who are substantially covered by their company, would also help reduce costs as workers would pay much closer attention to how their health dollars are spent. Today's average insurance bill paid by business is $833 according to The Kaiser Foundation. The worker pays the rest of costs, which averages $5,000 annually. Adding another $833 per month would be quite a financial shock. But transforming the health market will provide new insurance plans, new styles of paying for healthcare. The bite from transitioning old to new is not quite as bad as one would think, and in many cases financing quickly improves the worker's health finances.

Reshaping the Market

What should citizens expect of a government that proposes to manage the health care market instead of controlling it with government mandates and burdensome, expensive monopolies. First, look to the principles of liberal governance: faith, hard work, decentralized power, and liberty; and second understand the real problems in regarding America's health.

The first and foremost problem to remedy is that most politicians believe that the health care system is very different from other markets and requires the heavy hand of government. This is both arrogant and foolish. Every market is different. Retail is different from manufacturing. Gas and oil is different from Technology. The software business is different from the chocolate business. But all businesses are alike in that market forces ultimately determine the success or failure of any company or market. Health care is no different. Services delivered cost money. Charge too little and the provider is out of business. If value or quality is minimized, customers flee. Even in today's highly-regulated environments, cost cutting will produce poor quality which will ultimately prove deadly to any provider, government or private.

The health markets were perverted during World War II when the government placed wage controls on business as an inflation preventative. Tight labor markets demanded some mechanism to attract labor to war factories and the relief came in the form of tax free benefit - business provided health insurance becoming the centerpiece. That business-sponsored healthcare saw the light of day came only as a result of Harry Truman floating a national health insurance program that the unions loved but found little political support. (Health and Human Services, 2011)

Prior to Truman's allowance for business provided health insurance, nearly everyone paid for their own healthcare. Today, about 15% of Americans pay for their health needs with cash. These potential buyers of Cadillac health insurance are the citizens who opted out of the very costly in solution and opted in for cash. These are also the target of Obamacare. It should be noted that 'The uninsured are disproportionately between the ages of 18 and 34,' according to the Health and Human Services Administration. These are the predominately healthy young Americans who do not necessarily need health insurance nor feel the need to purchase the expensive HMO/PPO policy and have opted to pay cash. Obamacare's mean-spirited economics will use penalties to mandate purchases of insurance who believe Obamacare not a good investment. The funds from these new premium enlistees or tax penalties won't be for their benefit but will be used to pay for shortfalls in Medicare and Medicaid. This means more cost-shifting, just in a more sinister way.

The ultimate result, Americans have no idea what the cost of their health care is, so there in little focus on value. With little focus on value, less value is placed on health behavior which today translates into increased incidences or cancer, obesity and numerous other chronic conditions, driving up the cost of healthcare for business and government.   Government intrusion is ruining our health.

To build a market from scratch from the ashes of the very poorly run government and insurance monopolies, the foundation must begin with sound principles of governance and a very keen understanding of the long term objectives. What follows is a list ideas that are proposed more for debate than as a permanent resolve:

Mission

- Flatten or reduce health care costs by improving the individual health of all Americans

Strategies:

- Personalize Health Financing to Match the Trend toward Personalized Healthcare
- End business provided health benefits and government monopolies
- Assure no harm to for clients with pre-existing issues and seniors enrolled in Medicare

Tactics: Liberal Governance

- Liberty: Vastly increase financing choices for individuals by deregulating insurance industry
- Personal Responsibility: Allow insurance rating based on personal health behavior, both good and bad behavior
- Reduced Government: Replace federal health monopolies with market solutions

- Hard Work: End requirements for hours-worked or dollars earned for Obamacare and Medicaid will reduce number of part time workers. New dollars saved from market solutions will be available for investment in business and new job creation and help the lower quadrant of income earners to earn more money.
- Faith and reason: No more government mandates for The Pill

Though it is impossible to say what creative entrepreneurs in the insurance industry might invent for financing, a few solutions are likely.

- Whole life policies that have a specific lifetime payout that are available in large denominations, say in increments of $100,000. A typical American accrues about $250,000 in healthcare costs in a life time.
- Customized healthcare plans: perhaps hospitalization only policies as hospital costs are generally a big ticket item. Alternatively, specialist policies - as big ticket doctors outside of the general practitioner are high cost physicians. Insurance companies could cobble together a set of practices into a policy.
- High deductible policies of $10,000, $15,000, and $30,000 that are coupled with an HSA feature where unused dollars could be rolled into succeeding years, building a cash care nest egg
- Insurance rating that includes health behavior as factor as well as age and sex
- HMO and PPO: Some of the rich will just pay cash for healthcare, because it is far less expensive that an insurance solution, others will prefer the old style solutions like the HMO/PPO. Unions will not likely wish to give up this Cadillac solution for their minions.
- Catastrophic cost coverage: As an optional coverage, a person might wish to have protection against the possibility of contracting a chronic disease that requires great cost to ameliorate.

Personal Healthcare: Ending Business Provided Health Insurance

Change is never easy. Breaking up AT&T made many customers grumble. Ending health insurance as a tax-free business benefit will be no different. Understanding what lay on the other side of this transformational change will help ease the fear of citizens and the hysteria in which the Left and Right will likely engage. The first and foremost result of personalizing healthcare and health responsibility will be that health costs will diminish. Why? Moving from a series of health monopolies – Medicare, Medicaid, Obamacare, and Business provided (highly regulated, one-size fits all insurance via HMO/PPO) – to personalized, lightly regulated, cash-based routine care will reduce costs. When patients pay for services from their own cash, the amount of unneeded care will drop, costly tests abate, and the cost for services will become very competitive. Insurance will focus on the expensive health issues.

The Probable Cost of Insurance

First, for those of us who are insured by the business, ending business provided insurance will mean a pay raise – and not an insubstantial one. The pay raise will be very competitive and will likely cover much or all of individual and family health costs, for some there will be money left over. The pay raise will be sizable because every company will want to keep their employees. This pay raise will show up as not just a bigger check, but it is more than likely to show up as a separate line item not as a benefit but as a highlight of what that benefit is. Many in Congress will wish to mandate what this percentage is, but this is old-style, Leftist thinking. Mandating a percentage would eliminate competition. Competition will drive the percentage up, for everyone. Mandates will fix the pay raise and assure that no one ever receives a higher payout.

Second, the cost of insurance will drop.   Less expensive financing solutions will sideline the HMO/PPO for the rich and union members (a favored political class), cost-shifting will decline as government monopolies will come to an end of life via creative destruction, and better health behavior will result because of health behavior rating for policies. All but a small percentage of patients will favor better health over higher premiums. Those unwilling to change their behavior will pay higher premiums, as they should.

Three examples will help validate that market-based solutions will accomplish cost savings and improve health behavior which in turn will improve health.   They are 1) what the 'average' family working for a large business would pay for coverage using current PPO costs with the expected reductions produced by a less regulated market, 2) what insurance is available for a family of 4 working for a small business and a head of household that is 40, and 3) a Medicaid client costs versus a market solution. The primary difference for the first two options is that large companies tend to currently pay a bigger portion of insurance costs than small companies and also pay employees better as well.

Typical Family working for Large Business

The Kaiser Family foundation publishes a variety of research for the healthcare industry. For the typical family with two kids and a wife their employer pays, on average, $15,000 according to the Foundation. (The Kaiser Family Foundation, 2012) Of this amount the company pays a bit over $10,000 leaving about $5000 to the employee which includes part of the premium and whatever routine healthcare cost are accrued via copayments and coinsurance.

The cost the average insurance policy (Kaiser Foundation) purchased for this typical family is about $15,000 a year or $1,266 per month. This cost is inflated, as discussed earlier, in three ways 1) government cost shifting accounts for an estimated 15%, 2) costs associated with poor health behavior which accounts for another 15%

and probably more, and 3) taxes paid for Medicare (1.45% of the average income of $52,762 (Census Bureau) or $63.75 per month, and Medicaid costs which come directly from the general fund and cost the taxpayer about $117 per month and rising quickly.

For a healthy person, these reductions in the cost of the monthly premium of $1,266 reduce the new market premium to $705.85. During the transition from business-provided healthcare to personally purchased healthcare, most every company will provide a pay raise. Companies that really want to keep their employees will pay more. Others will scrimp. It is likely that 60% of the payouts for insurance will be paid out as a pay raise. The more competitive the markets for employees the higher the percentage. At 60%, the pay raise will be $759.95 which would cover the estimated cost ($705.85) of the very expensive HMO/PPO in our new free-market solution. But few will not opt for the expensive solution.

Most will purchase a high-deductible, low coinsurance plan with an HSA. Plans will vary, but a $10,000 deductible can be found on eHealthinsurance for about one-third of the cost of the high cost HMO/PPO. So for $253.32 (this without any deductions for cost shifting so it is inflated) a plan can be purchased leaving $506.63 per month from the healthcare raise from the company for out of the pocket expenses. Patients will preserve the flow of health cash and carefully mete out dollars assuring even more health care savings. For those Americans who are healthy, a larger amount of the monthly stipend will be saved for future expenses. For those who have poor health behaviors they will either acquire better habits or they will pay a premium for continued poor behavior. As stated in the Safeway example above, few wanted to pay the additional premium for poor health habits and they changed their behavior. For those with chronic illnesses or genetic diseases like cancer, where good health behavior does not fully mitigate disease, catastrophic coverage and gap policy coverage will per part of the collage of solutions available in the market.

The $506.63 also measures another metric, one for government incompetence. This number reflects the ineffective nature of a command and control system which constrains personal freedom. As markets mature in this new health care world, the portion of $506.63 not spent on healthcare will be a measure of the efficiencies of personal responsibility.

Average Joe Working for a Small Business

Average Joe's example may be more in line with the 'real' typical American as it is difficult to believe that the typical median income worker earns $44,000 a year works for a business that funds a $15,000 insurance policy. Could be wrong, but to error on the side of good judgment, this example highlights what a typical person working for a small business (one they might own) may find when pricing an HMO/PPO in the new, less regulated environment. Again, the example policy will be an 80/20 insurance/coinsurance, and $2000 deductible policy with low co-pays. Using eHealthInsurance, a very popular and well-known blue insurance company posted a policy for $783.00 per month (May 2013). A $10,000 deductible policy was available and 20% coinsurance after deductible $282.56 per month. Additionally, instead of deducting $117 for estimated Medicaid taxes, as effective tax rates progressively reduce the dollars taken from Average Joe's paycheck, this number is halved to $58.50. Using these numbers, and reducing the burden government places on each of us as well as accounting for good health behavior rating, the costs in the new market-based world are $425.85 for the Cadillac HMO/PPO and $136.98 for the high-deductible policy.

If Average's Joe's company give Joe's a raise of just half of the original policy cost (noting that bigger companies with high pay rates will likely pay the previously quoted 60% of the health costs) of $783 per month or $391.50, this would be close to paying for the expensive HMO/PPO solution of $425. But Joe is a smart guy, though our leaders may not think so, and Joe will opt or the $136.94 high-deductible policy leaving him $2,760 a year to pay out of pocket expenses.

For the chronically ill who have good health behavior, the HMO/PPO will be a better fit. A much better fit. For those Americans who decided that poor health behavior is their desire state of freedom, like a reckless driver they will pay more, probably progressively more.

Medicaid

Medicaid recipients, who get no help from anyone but the government, acquire on average Medicaid benefits averaging $4350 for each adult and $2441 for each child. If this seems a bit expensive, it is. This cohort generally has the fewest opportunities to work, generally because of the lack of education provided in government schools. This cohort has the greatest hardship and generally does not have the best health behavior. The two greatest factors that will help improve the health of this cohort, and reduce the cost of healthcare is 1) improving education (addressed shortly) and 2) reducing poor health behavior by allowing rating for health behavior, including rating for pregnancy, or offering policies with or without childbirth. Over 500,000 births in 2009 were paid for by Medicaid per the Kaiser Foundation. As illegitimacy is very high nationally (40%) and much higher in cities and inner cities, it is very likely that Medicaid is funding easily over one half of these births with no father present, adding a fifth element to poor health behavior, pregnancy and the single mom. That single parentage is an additional poor health behavior, one must understand that a single mother, that is a mother with no father present, and child are at significant economic disadvantages which generally translates into instant poverty. This hardship exacerbates difficulties with education and health. Per the Centers for Disease Control in Atlanta:

'Children and adults in families with income below or near the federal poverty level have worse health than those with higher income (see Appendix II, Poverty, for a definition of the federal poverty level). Although in some cases illness can lead to poverty, more often poverty causes poor health by its connection with inadequate nutrition, substandard housing, exposure to environmental hazards, unhealthy lifestyles, and decreased access to and use of health care services'. (Centers for Disease Control, 2007, p. 41)

The health expenses of those living in poverty are high not because they are sicker genetically or simply because they are poor but because of poor behaviors and the gifting of health financing by the government for which the rating system on health behavior is neutral. It costs little or nothing to be sick. There is no requirement to improve behavior to reduce the potential for disease. That government has extended a hand to help has actually harmed the people it is trying to help. Though more on welfare will come shortly, having access to less expensive private insurance that can be rated for the four key health behaviors plus pregnancy is a good starting place for welfare reform. If the current government health care system is encouraging child bearing and poor health behavior for single parents, then disincentives for this conduct will help the overall health of those in poverty by removing one primary cause of poverty in the United States, single-parent families.

Were Medicaid clients to seek high deductible health insurance in the new marketplace, using the same costing mechanisms above, a single man or women in their twenties with good health behavior, insurance would run about $50 per month or about $0.25 an hour or less. Even for the worker flipping burgers this is affordable, more affordable that Obamacare. At $0.50 an hour, they could build an HSA nest egg during the healthful youth years. A family working at minimum wage would have about the same costs, just combined. Family planning would work a bit different for either the two-earner versus single earner. Financing pregnancy and childbirth would have to be planned either by building up an HSA account or saving for the big event and purchasing a policy that included childbearing. Gone would be the government's financing of single parent families.

For those who choose poor health behavior, higher cost would be incurred as an incentive to get healthy.

Summary

If markets change the landscape of healthcare, the oceans will neither rise nor the sky's fall if implemented, and the very high costs we now pay for government incompetence would result in the building of HSA nest eggs for the vast majority of people. If better health is the mission of our nation, then opening the insurance rating system to include health behavior would improve and reduce costs. Sending both government and businesses reliance on the HMO/PPO Cadillac to the ash heap of history would add significant cost reductions and would end the tyranny of government subsidized insurance and remedy the economic crutch of business provided insurance.

Is there political will to transform our healthcare system? Will Democrats give up their notion that government is a better steward of our health than its citizens? Do Republicans really believe in free markets? Will citizens rise up and demand better health care? The answer is no, no and no, but change is never easy and this new venture shouldn't be broadly executed anyway. This should be a solution meted out by the states, perhaps just a couple for comparison and debate's sake, say Oklahoma, a relatively moderate state, and Massachusetts, which already has ObamneyCare which mandates the purchase of Cadillac insurance policies for all. Personalizing health care will have some rough edges to smooth, but the end product will improve healthcare and reduce costs as well. There may be a chance that a market solution will fail, which is good. That benefit of liberal governance is that failure will lead to better solutions. Even a satisfactory solution will need to be improved and having 50 states as incubators is a fabulous landscape to build best practices. With objectives set to measure success and a quality improvement process in place, it is very likely that total savings over time will be better than stated here.

Efficiency Four: Example: Reorganizing Retirement

Medicare is the 800-pound gorilla of healthcare and of federal budget busters. With Social Security as its sister monopoly, a combined *unfunded* mandate of $44 trillion lay squarely on the backs of our children and grandchildren. The financial challenge is so great that even doubling Social Security and Medicare taxes may not provide the needed tax revenue to close the funding gap.

Leftists challenge any attempted changes in either Medicare or Social Security as a change that would also threaten current beneficiaries, which is non-sense in reality, though it is very powerful marketing. Regardless, no solution should leave millions of retirees to fend for themselves. This is hardly a realistic solution. Making adjustment to assure that the promises of these retirees are met is a key requirement of any transformation to a market-based solution. Because this is essential, any solution requires a forty-year transition period with a two-pronged approach that allows current workers to save for retirement and current retirees a smooth reform solution that doesn't burst the bank, theirs or the government's.

Though the government should have never made financial promises it could not keep: nearly limitless free healthcare and pensions for every citizen based on continually rising tax rates from working citizens, it did. The last 10 Congresses while knowing a gigantic fiscal crisis was brewing simple kicked the can down the road and did nothing to transform the current set of crippled solutions. During the 2012 election, when the crush of Medicare and Social Security was evident to most every citizen, solutions were barely mentioned. For Obama, fixing these programs was simply not on his agenda, and the only person with a plan, Paul Ryan's fixed benefit program for Medicare, has been lampooned by Democrats, and received a cool shoulder from many Republicans. So our Federal promise blissful retirement is still in place, just without the money to back the promise.

Wisely, FDR did negotiate with Congress to assure Social Security would be funded by its own tax to assure Social Security checks sent to retirees was funded by this revenue stream only. In a way, it was a PayGo solution, just 80 years earlier than today's Congressional rendition. To assure outlays were in fact covered Social Security taxes only, taxes have increased from 1% to 6.4% over the last 70 years, and with shortfalls now occurring, taxes should rise again. Medicare also has a separate tax of 1.45%, but there was no such pressure to make sure that payouts do not exceed tax revenue. Medicare has been short funding for some time and running deficits. Social Security and Medicare taxes have not risen though. They have not risen since the 1990s after having been raised over 20 times since their inceptions (1937 and 1967 respectively), because there is little public support for these already very high tax rates.

In the past, Social Security tax revenues far exceeded expenditures, and Congress simply spent the overage on whatever it pleased and left and IOU in the till. Now that tax revenues do not meet required outlays, dollars are allocated (that's a polite term) from the general fund. FDR's Paygo solution has simply been tossed to the curb. The dollars required to cover the shortfall are not chump change. Both programs required an additional $350 billion in revenues in 2012 and the amount taken from the general fund is growing rapidly. PayGo for these programs is long since dead. Doubling taxes over the next 20 years would almost cover the gap, but there has been no legislative initiative for this solution for obvious reasons. Citizens would revolt. Ditto for raising the retirement age, or mean-testing, or just about any solution that might help.

To assure these programs do not cannibalize federal constitution responsibilities and to assure future and current retirees get benefits, both reform and transformation are required; reform so that medical costs can be contained, and pensions funded, and transformation because an intergenerational tax as configured will never work without significant, perpetual tax increases.

Giving Americans a choice of how to save for requirement and when to retire are the backbone of creating significant wealth and freedom for all Americans.   So as a government monopoly with few choices has not work, will a Liberal solutions with more freedom and no monopoly work? Most assuredly.

Step One: Reform Medicare, Then Transform

'Not one of these, our citizens, should ever be abandoned to the indignity of charity.' (Johnson, 1965) That the very Leftist LBJ thought charity was undignified should leave the reader speechless, as charity is a crucial underpinning of our cultural greatness. It is unlikely that LBJ meant Medicare to be a charity replacement, but simply another monopoly to provide services he believed we could not provide for ourselves.

President Johnson also said during the speech that retirees desired the best health care available. It should be no surprise that America's quality of health care truly is second to none, but *best* is an adjective which best defines private healthcare not government healthcare. As Johnson was incorrect about charity being undignified, he was also wrong government provided healthcare as the best solution available.

Understanding what is amiss in Medicare is essential to understanding how to fix it. These deficiencies also apply to Social Security

- Each program is a centralized solution based on a one-sized fits all product; the left's principle - favoring equality over choice and liberty
- Medicare and Social Security monopolies presume that all Americans are unable to fend for themselves regarding both determining when to retire and how to fund retirement
- A nearly immobile and fixed retirement age is at odds with life expectancy that has been increasing steadily for centuries.

The discussion of the efficiencies of a free market solution, where providers compete for client's dollars with a variety of value solutions, has already been discussed. Government social monopolies are simply a less efficient device for allocating precious resources. Why government funding mechanisms have failed for these programs is simple – an intergenerational tax solution is unsustainable as the retirement population is increasing as lifespans increase, and decreasing family sizes assures a smaller population of tax payers. The current financing system is based on four faulty variables; 1) an intergenerational tax (from workers' pay to retiree benefits), 2) life expectancy that has been increasing steadily for over two hundred years accelerating rapidly last century and potential equally as rapidly this century and next, and, 3) the cost of health care which has been increasing faster than GDP for some time and will continue for the foreseeable future, and 4) family size that has steadily decreased over the last 80 years and is still decreasing.

The Social Security Administration correctly estimates that Social Security and Medicare taxes must rise to nearly 15% from 7.65% to pay for the estimated $44 trillion shortfall expected over the next 40 years. Since the Reagan administration this solution has never been discussed in Congress. No leader has put pen to paper to produce a House or Senate bill for discussion or debate of a tax solution for our retirement programs.

An alternative to tax increases is a reduction of ever increasing population of retirees, expected to reach 86 million by 2050 from 40 million today. Raising the retirement age would help reduce this number of retirees and this solution has both been discussed and legislated. For those born after 1960 the retirement age has been raised to 67 years. Any senior citizen can opt to retire at 62. These Social Security checks are paid at a lower rate that full retirement at 65 or 67. But even if everyone retired at 67, the effect on the budget gap over the next 40 years is only minuscule. The 115% rise of retirees over the next 40 years occurs as the general population is expected to increase only 46%. The result: fewer workers paying taxes to support the elderly. Looking into the future this number never gets better, not ever, because the retirement age is nearly fixed, and life expectancy will continue to increase, for...ever!

Had FDR and his Brain Trust connected the retirement age to life expectancy, our financing problem vaporizes. Average life expectancy in 1940 when Ida May Fuller received the very first Social Security payout of $22.54, was 65.2 years for women. Today, had retirement been pegged to life expectancy, which according to the World Bank is 78.2 years for Americans, most of our financing issues would be dramatically reduced.

Using Census tables as the reference, the number of citizens over 65 is 40.2 million. Those over 79 account for only 9.4 million. Funding Social Security and Medicare for this small population would reduce our current costs by about 75% and produce significant surpluses. Congress might even see fit to reduce taxes, perhaps as low as 3%, allowing for citizens to save more for retirement. Congress might even consider means testing that could reduce government burden even more, allowing the tax rate for float further down toward 2%. This, of course, is a pipe dream.

Increasing the retirement age, though is highly unlikely, and to pair it to life expectancy, well, even less likely. Like raising taxes, this palliative is unlikely. Pegging the retirement age to life expectancy still does not fix Medicare as much of the costs of this program occur in the last two years of a person's life. Medicare costs are accelerating and regulators have only two answers; pay providers less and diminish quality and increase cost shifting, or reduce the kinds and types of procedures available to patients via what Sarah Palin calls death panels. The difficulty with artificially constraining costs and benefits is that the end game is sadly poor quality and diminishing access to resources. As with most monopolies, after the first day of their economic existence, neither quality nor value ever improves.

There is a better way. It is a two-step process. First, provide a fixed-benefit solution for Medicare (a la RyanCare), and, second, personalize Medicare and Social Security by transforming an intergenerational tax system into savings/investment solution. A fixed benefit solution aligns Medicare to Social Security's fixed benefit solution and makes a transformation to a personalized solution much smoother.

Although there may be many options for a fixed benefit solution, something like Paul Ryan has proposed and passed by the House of Representatives in 2011, is a good solution with which to start a debate. Ryan's reform path increases personal responsibility and heightens freedom of choice as the dollars can be used to purchase insurance in the open market. Coupled with good behavior rating, high-deductible insurance could be purchased with cash left over for routine care. The Ryan bill allots $14,000 a year to purchase insurance and healthcare; many may purchase an HMO/PPO. Others will invest in a high-deductible solution that, for a 64 year-old, should cost around $400 per month. Note: insurance premiums for those who are 65 or older are not available because Medicare, mandated to acquire the Social Security benefit, makes private insurance obsolete for anyone over 65.

Mr. Ryan's solution still retains the government-run, social monopoly in place and inevitably, if left in place, would succumb to problems caused by a continual increasing expectancy for longer lives. It does however provide the two tools necessary to transition for personalized retirement, one with few legal strictures enacted by government. First, the costs for a fixed benefit solution are easier to manage than an unlimited benefit, and, second, opening the private market for insurance allows competition that increases the possibility for further cost reductions for all retirees.

Step Two: Transformation

What are the nuts and bolts of a Liberal Transformation away from a government-based, one-size-fits-all social retirement monopoly? What gives America's citizens more freedom, more choices, and a better life? The answer is both simple enough for a fifth grader to understand and so frightening that most Leftist's first pale, then rail, at the suggestion. The answer is a simple habit that Americans have traditionally done very well and that our Chinese competitors do at the rate of 50%, they save. Most anyone would easily answer 'yes' to the following question. 'Do you want to be taxed 7.65% on every dollar you earn, or would you rather save it for retirement?'

The proposed framework should contain several elements:

- Savings/Investment accounts need to insure threshold for investments return. Accounts should not contain high risk investments but assure returns in the 4.5% to 6% return. Institutions who do not consistently meet these investments goals would lose their right to participate.
- Individuals will determine when to retire.
- During the transition from fully-government run to fully-personalized retirement, Congress should consider raising the retirement age for those, issuing special bonds for paying underfunding of Social Security and Medicare costs for those currently in the system, and means testing of benefits.
- New savings for workers over the next 5, 10 to 40 years will reduce the dependence of government help, a government check during retirement, and allow the termination of the program in three or four decades. These new retirement savings will make much of America very rich. (Using information about my social security and Medicare tax deductions over the last four decades and applying a 4.5% rate of return, my nest egg would be $1.5 million – and I am by no means a rich man.)

The first and most important goal of this program is to assure that the government causes no harm to those who have the most need.

Does a personal savings program help or hurt those with the least resources? Using the worst case example, a person making minimum wage their whole working life, from 16 to 76 (just an FYI, life expectancy will be higher than 76 in 60 years...), even using the minimum wage before it was recently raised, $7.25 an hour, and assuming only an average 2.5% annual increase of wages, a person who never receives the financial benefit of marriage and earns an average of 5.5% per annum on their investments, would save $795,899 (includes the value of a mobile home) dollars. If the person purchased a well-worn mobile home and property for $50,000, it would be worth as estimated $230,000 (assuming 3% annual asset appreciation.)

How does this nest egg translate into a more easily understood value based on today's dollars? The person's purchasing power would decline by an eight according to MeasuringWorth.com. Assuming an average life expectancy for a person 65 who is in the bottom half of America's earner is about 16 years, (Social Security Administration, 2007) then an annuity with a principle of $570,000 paying out over 16 years would produce a monthly payment in today's dollars of would be $6,458.20 per month divided by the Measuringworth.com deflator of a factor of 8, results in monthly payments of $807.35.   Today's payout of about $587 per month, plus Medicare exceeds their expected payout from a personalized savings solution, so these low-earners (about two percent of the population) would likely need some assistance. Selling his home at some point would further help his finances, but having a home to live in may be more important than having the cash unless there is an end of life crisis. This group is small enough that it is likely that between charities and family, government intervention would cause more problems than successes. More important, this is the group that new and workable social welfare policies will rise up, and, if well designed, erase the cultural and social problems that cause them financial hardship. But more on this shortly.

For the median American Family, retirement changes dramatically, given the same metrics, but starting at the median income (in 2000) of $42,128, savings after 60 years accumulate to $2.3 million. The $150,000 starter home's value has increased to over $600,000. Moving to a smaller home and netting the difference in equity of $300,000, then depreciating future savings by a factor of 8 to obtain what that's savings payout might look like today, the median family nets about $30,000 a year without touching their assets, while today's median income retiree nets only about $1149 per month or $14,000 a year. Because today's retirees cannot afford quite as nice a home, as the above savers, due to the high taxation for Social Security and Medicare, their appreciated asset will not likely produce nearly the benefit.

With a savers solution, then, except for a few, everyone is better off including the millions of additional jobs created by the $75 to $100 trillion in investible income that businesses will enable America to expand and innovate. The biggest unintended consequence may be that we save too much. But this issue is far easier to deal with than the looming $44 trillion dollar deficit caused by our intergenerational tax solution.

A highly expected and yet unintended benefit results from health care as innovation provides a path to fully Personalized Healthcare. Over the next 30 years innovations in genomics and proteomics will generate new procedures that allow physicians and pharmaceutical companies to create cures on the fly, cures that are designed and produced for a specific, individual genome. Influenza will disappear as a doctor will have technology to create a one-off flu vaccine that is built both for your genome and is a perfect antidote for the flu contracted by the patient. Ditto for diseases like cancer, hypertension, Alzheimer's, dementia, and, for that matter, any disease. Skin cells taken from your body will be able to help regrow diseased tissue for bones, heart and even the brain. The final frontier, aging, will be solved or at very least mitigated with genomic updates allowing for small changes that extend the life of our cells. The result, after the technology is commoditized, probably well before mid-century, the cost of health care will drop like a rock. Life-saving cancer treatments will be available at your local Walgreen's or perhaps right in your doctor's office.

With Personalized retirement, government intrusion into our retirement decisions would end. A person that is terminally ill at 45 will have a nest egg available so assure the best lifestyle possible for the end of life but also to assure his family's future. As life expectancy increases, so too will our likely age of retirement.

This transformation will be a challenge as half of social security revenues will be going into individual citizen's savings accounts instead of into the treasury to pay retiree benefits. This chunk of lost revenue will need to come from mean-testing, incremental increases in retirement age, and purchases of Social Security and Medicare Bonds as part of the Savers investment portfolio and an increasing large investment portfolio that will be taxed as Savers retire. There may be bumps along the way, but this solution will be far less expensive than trying to find revenues to cover the $44 trillion in unfunded mandates where there is no likelihood of tax increases.

Having access to the Social Security Administration's significantly better demographics and computing would allow a better and very exacting answer for the question 'is the *Saver* path a less expensive than the current tax-based solution?' The simple answer is 'Yes.' The exact answer is less clear. Without the luxury of the government's extensive demographics, an educated guess is that underfunded transition costs will be $15 to $20 trillion over the next 25 years, give or take $5 trillion. Budget surpluses should occur in about 20 years as the majority new retirees will have produced nest eggs that require no financial input from the government. A wise government would, at this juncture, begin reducing the 7.65% businesses pay in Social Security and Medicare taxes. With at least $75 trillion in new assets to tax and with savings from personalizing Medicaid, Obamacare, and, to be discussed shortly, Welfare, a net savings to the Federal budget will occur. These savings and reapportioning of responsibilities back to the States and the Citizens, total federal taxation could drop below 10 percent.

Efficiency Five: Personalized Social Welfare

U.S. Senator Joseph S. Clark, Jr., Mayor of Philadelphia described the modern "liberal" position very frankly in these words:

'To lay a ghost at the outset and to dismiss semantics, a liberal is here defined as one who believes in utilizing the full force of government for the advancement of social, political, and economic justice at the municipal, state, national, and international levels.' (Clark, 1953)

Well, the Christian part of Leftist ideas aside, Joe was trying to steal the likeable branding of Liberal and associate the moniker with Leftist thinking which had taken quite a beating from its political linkage to Socialism, National Socialism (Fascism), Progressivism, Statism, and a whole range of *the state rules* political thinking. Quite sadly the Left took a really great notion, Liberal Democracy, and over the course of 80 years trashed its beautiful meaning. Even its most pedestrian definition Liberal meant plentiful or open-minded, also a notion the Left has never remotely adopted.

Regardless, liberal notions of freedom and personal responsibility were quickly retread as government responsibility for personal financial welfare. Because 'the man,' the man being the terrible and awful capitalist that would only pay someone what they were worth and not a penny more, was holding back the proletariat, the Left, big government must be the enforcer, the check writer for those in need. From FDR through today, our social policy has been based on making up any real or imagined financial discrepancy for the poor and not so poor by writing checks and chits for which no value is returned. Society has not gotten better, nor has the plight of the poor improved. For those who receive checks, character, work ethic, honor, loyalty, ethical behavior, and duty have not improved. Money will not buy an improvement in any these elements which are crucial to human success. And most certainly, money *can't buy them love.*

The trail of devastation from this intellectually empty philosophy has crippled education in the inner city, prevented the natural processes that lead to marriage, reduced the work ethic, increased joblessness, reduced connections to church and civic organizations. In short, our social welfare policies have created a permanent underclass that has little or no opportunity to access the delights of the American Dream.

And yet the Left calls these notions *Enlightened Government* and Republicans traipse along with the Democrats as though the 'give a man a fish' social policy is good government. Go figure.

What is good social policy? What works? Ninety-eight of Americans who participate in four traditional social programs that are as old as Noah and only one requires funding, the others needing no help from government. Better yet, these social programs are almost universally accepted as highly beneficial for both the individual and the state. One might wonder how it seem remotely possible that for decades these programs have escaped the learned eyes of our elected officials? But they have. The Left will be astonished that these *Leave it to Beaver* solutions work. But they do. They are not, however, enlightened according to the Left, but they do indeed work and if you are a problem solver looking for solutions that work, and their success is hard to overlook. Though most anyone with even a lick of sense, even peoples that predate Noah, will testify to the efficacy of these solutions, they have been largely ignored.

What are the four social programs? They are the traditional pillars of personal success:

- Education; acquire as much education as possible, free or otherwise
- Acquire a job, two or three if necessary to assure your lifestyle in a way that is concomitant to your needs
- Get married and stay married, knowing that what you give is far greater than what you get in life, and your wife/husband and children will be the better for it

- Attend church, or join a civic organization, and commit to doing something bigger and greater than your own life by helping others

These are simple solutions that have met the test of time and produce great results and have for centuries. Except for education (another government social monopoly that needs to be broken up and will be discussed later) none of these require a tax or government regulation. With Social Security and Medicare personalized, government really has no business in marriage except via the states when determining how estates might be divvied up.

These are personal welfare programs because each builds character, integrity, work ethic, relationship building, personal responsibility, personal accountability...and a litany of other personal achievement capabilities. A check from the government does none of these, just a giving a man a fish does little. When a citizen is in the need of financial resources, generally lack of money is a symptom, not a core problem.

Personal Welfare reform really does translate into creating Great Americans.

Education is the Crucial Pillar for Personal Success

So what is missing from our culture, our society that assures the uplifting of bottom chunk of our society (about 25% of Americans.) Change starts with unchaining lowest performers from the bondage of government schools and government welfare programs that absolutely assure inter-generational poverty. The first step, in the four step Liberal welfare reform is education. Without a quality education this slice of America is crippled, assuring that our four-cylinder Ferrari economy runs only on three cylinders. Why? Education increases the value of an individual's hard work with better pay and creates the right financial basis for marriage, for both the man and the woman. A woman is less likely to choose a man that can't provide for a family, and a man is less likely to marry until he can provide for a family. With a low population of educated men predominate in this lower income quadrant, many women choose single-family parentage, which leads to a life of financial stress and government dependence. Education, then, is the cornerstone of personal success because it leads to more valuable work, then a much higher rate of marriage and hopefully more time in charitable endeavors.

The continuous cycle of declining success, less education, fewer jobs and more illegitimacy, is creating a larger and more permanent underclass. Progressive social policy is the culprit. A new Liberal education is the first step for transforming social policy.

So why can't we educate everyone well. There are two immense problems, ones common to all social monopolies that dispense goods or services for free. First, there is no exchange of value. This is a duplication of the problems associated with government healthcare and the one-size-fits-all HMO/PPO insurance policy. The person acquiring the education benefit has no idea what the cost is and may not care because no dollars leave their wallet. The fewer taxes one pays, the more education is viewed as an entitlement. For the poor, the cost of taxation is nearly invisible showing up in sales tax and the tax burden hidden in rent payments. Like most social programs and their associated tax, education becomes a prerogative, something expected from government, not necessarily valued as an important tool for life's success.

Over the course of 80 years as the government built a gigantic education monopoly and expanded social welfare monopolies, education is seen less and less as a pathway to personal success in the inner city. With a declining industrial base, a traditional career path for inner city residents, an education seems less and less important. Although schools have a vast array of quality issues with teachers, curriculum and government micromanagement, the fundamental problem is there is no apparent exchange of value such that a parent 1) would care that what they paid had value, and 2) had alternatives when that value was low. Put another way: parents don't write a check for the service each month or semester, and if they did pay for school, they would very much need alternatives when the current school of choice was not providing the education they desired.

Additionally, there is no contract, either implied or real. If a parent were paying for schooling, nothing is written to explain what value should be expected. From the school's viewpoint, no set of guidelines are codified as to what is expected of the student.

State and Federal mandates for testing achievement have helped gauge success and provide a roadmap to teachers for what should be included in curriculum. The most important teacher in this equation, the parent(s), have been excluded from the education process. Worse, both teachers and parents are not held accountable. Teachers who are poor teachers cannot be fired. Parents have no list of student duties for which they are help contractually accountable. Lack of accountability for both teacher and parent, and the fact that no dollars exchange hands, break the foundation of education and assure poor results except for the very motivated parent, student and teacher – a very small population.

Without parent and teacher accountability, without a contract with consequences for non-compliance to the contract, and without choices for both the parent and school when the contract is broken, no amount of dollars spent on education will improve education.

Liberal education (not Leftist) demands an equal and fair exchange of value between parent and school, the student and the teacher. Three items are missing from a today's Leftist solution: 1) a contract with responsibilities and recourse for each party, 2) an abundance of choices when contractual obligations are not met, and 3) dollars (whether real or in the form of a voucher) to weigh the value of the exchange; i.e. money has to exchange hands in this transaction.

Dollars for parents to purchase an education should be available for any school, private, religious, charter, online, whatever. Schools should be shuttered for non-performance. Financing private and religious schools could be a bit of a sticky wicket. Should government dollars be spent to sponsor any or all religions? Should Islamist schools be allowed to teach a curriculum which would likely be very anti-American, anti-liberty? If not, how do we countenance the First Amendment? These challenges are easily resolved - at the state level. If a secular curriculum is recommended by the state, then vouchers are for the secular content proposed by the recommendations, and only that content. Preaching is for Sundays. Content and character are for the classroom. The state shouldn't pay for any religious content.

Reducing the federal government's total responsibility in K-12 is the second step to improving education. Fed duties should be limited to two obligations: establishing benchmarks for each grade and identifying best practices for teaching each subject. In that the government has become highly political in its endeavors to craft educational guidelines, even two responsibilities may be too many, but the threshold must be set somewhere. These limited responsibilities are a good start.

Finally, states should have no more responsibilities than the federal government, setting benchmarks for each grade and writing vouchers to parents. Monopoly powers of individual school districts should be pared back as well, allowing each school to stand on its own and to find inventive solutions to help them compete with private options. Their representation of teachers has left the children and parents unrepresented. At very least, unions membership and dues deductions should not be mandatory. Teachers should have rights to representation as they see fit, not mandated by Leftist rules by the state. As co-conspirators with the government in their allied effort to spend more money regardless of results, they have continually harmed the ability of schools to educate our children. Their efforts have traditionally run quite counter to the execution of a quality education. Instead of increasing the freedom of teachers to teach, their one-size-fits-all approach to education and union membership has debilitated the efforts to modernize our schools.

Although some improvements in educational achievement will be immediate, poor performance is a generational problem. It takes 13 years for a kindergartener to move through each grade and graduate. It takes 20 to 25 years for a person to mature, leverage a good education, acquire a good entry level job, and then perhaps a few more to find that magic person to create a family and start the process again.   Each new crop of children entering school need parents to leverage new innovations in education to get even more benefit. The whole process needs an Edward Deming infusion for continuous process improvement.   As the market opens and competition accelerates, poor curriculum will fade away, better teachers will be attracted to the profession, and poor teachers will find new professions. Most important poor schools will either go out of business or improve. The status quo will be terminated.

For those politicians that are faint of heart, the states should be encouraged to experiment with open markets. Some states will stick to Leftist governance and fail and spend much money trying to prove the State is needed to provide a good education. They will discover the State is only needed if a poor education is a desired outcome.

Beyond the transformation from social monopolies or market solutions, regulatory monopolies need the gentle hand of Liberal governance and the intellectual pillar of simplicity applied.

Then Jobs, Family and a Great Society

Having a better educated populace in inner city and the suburbs must be accompanied by additional jobs. America's 21st century, especially the Obama years, have been marked by meager job growth and vast numbers of workers giving up of finding work. Lack of jobs results from three gross, government incompetencies, 1) over-regulation or the threat of more regulation, 2) large deficits to fund an oversized government, 3) belief that a government job is more productive that a private job.   Regardless, there are not only not enough government jobs for full employment, there most certainly is a huge deficit of private jobs and will be until the government ceases to carry large deficits removing significant dollars (over a trillion in 2013) from potential private investment in American jobs.

For those who may believe the economy is getting better and the 2013 marks a tipping point in employment numbers, this notion could not be more false. The underlying variable not mentioned in the March 2013 (and not uncharacteristic of most month that year)

172

numbers, for instance, shows unemployment dipping to 7.6% with only 88,000 jobs created. About 190,000 jobs are required to keep up with population growth, so the 102,000 jobs deficit should have created an up tic in the unemployment rate, but over 600,000 citizens left the work force.

'Looked at another way, just 58.6% of Americans work today, down from 60.6% when Obama took office. The average over the previous two decades was 63%.

There are, for example, 6.8 million people who aren't in the labor force but would be if there were jobs available. That's up more than 1 million since the recovery started in June 2009. The number of long-term unemployed is still higher than it was 3-1/2 years ago — and it jumped more than 90,000 in February.' (Investor's Daily, 2013)

The significant new investment from personalizing Social Security and Medicare will help immensely, but transforming government for the onerous big brother to a managing partner in our endeavors to find quality employment for everyone is essential.

As education effectiveness increases and more investment is possible due to increased American savings from Personalized Retirement solution, more jobs and better jobs will be available and an uptick in marriage should result, moving the marriage rate from its current rate of 60% back toward the 98% rate in the early 1950s. Education is the lynchpin, though. All children and parents need choices to assure they can invest in a high quality education.

Efficiency Six: Measuring Success or Failure

Success is an accident unless there is a plan, and every plan should have measureable objectives of success. Our government has no plan for success. It has no measure for what great results are.

Great governance, regardless the style government (tyranny, kingdom or republic) is crucial for achieving great goals. Greatness cannot simply be a campaign slogan. It must be our national goal. In America, more than any nation in the world, greatness is a pervasive piece of our tradition and culture. To assure great results, Liberal government must set a specific measure for greatness, whether social, economic or cultural, so citizens are intelligently armed with information by which to vote. This responsibility has gone wanting. The vast majority of the political elite defend 2% GDP growth as acceptable or even good. Even 7%-8% unemployment is something Americans was promoted as acceptable results. These are not acceptable results, regardless of past failures.

Greatness is not easy to achieve and greatness is impossible to achieve where no bar for greatness exists. With no goals, any achievement may be deemed acceptable, which is precisely the state of affairs in American politics. Yet, lack of goals, lack of national performance standards is not a bad habit associated only with the Federal Government. Few State and Local governments measure performance. Notable exceptions like the City of Boston that have comprehensive strategy management solutions should be lauded. Boston is the exception, not the norm. Most government agencies live and die by hoping that tax revenues will increase. Budgets are created via a cost plus method - that is next year's budget is simply whatever last year's costs were plus some fictitious additional percentage of dollars that generally exceeds inflation plus population growth. Additional revenues are not based on performance. Government has not been good at managing results and has excelled at spinning the message when results are poor. Government is not alone in ignoring mediocrity. Many businesses consider modest growth a success. But there is a difference between business and government. The difference is simple, profits and failure.

Vast numbers of small businesses fail, largely because of their inability to understand what and how to measure their performance, and, more important, how to right a listing ship when things go badly. Large businesses that incorporate have a publically available income statements and balance sheets as a score cards, and this helps to identify the not so good from the poor, the good from the great. The not so good find new solutions to difficult problem or fail. Failure is a crucial component for business success. Those who cannot turn failure into success, fail. Businesses go bankrupt. When governments fail to succeed, they simply ask for more money.

Good businesses understand how to manage their financial affairs well enough to assure profitability. But good and great are very different adjectives. Great companies understand that only two or three key strategies need significant attention to produce great results. (Collins, 2001) Understandably, a few key strategic initiatives will filter down into the organization creating a broader set of metrics that support key strategies. But all businesses have one key ingredient, one key ingredient to success that government does not, failure. When failure is a variable, focus on the elements of success, measuring the elements of success becomes incredibly important. When failure is not a variable for producing success, as is with government, mediocrity may be the best result possible. If no one is monitoring results, if no one is establishes metrics for success, if politicos spin what results poor results as good results, then the American public has no scorecard to determine success. The result - even mediocrity can easily be spun as good results.

If poor results are the new normal, then big government is an acceptable corollary of the new notion of acceptable success. As described in Deficiencies', size does matter. The size of government is directly related to our collective ability to achieve economic, social and cultural greatness. As we have seen during the Obama tenure, the rising size of government has inhibited GDP growth, kept employment high and increased our indebtedness. Anything approaching a full economic recovery is considered likely only in the distant future. Although the economy has not failed, America is slouching to a recovery and any metric for greatness is but a faint dream in a very distant future.

The first step to success is establishing a grade card for key economic, social and cultural indicators. What rate of GDP growth is an A and what is an F. What rate of marriage is failing and what is passage and what will assure the foundation of a great society. Understanding what grades are required to achieve greatness in just a few metrics such as GDP, educational attainment, employment and marriage rate will give great insight to whether our government's size and scope of responsibilities are in line with greatness.

What is Just Right size for government? What size will allow American's to achieve both personal and national greatness? Does our government need to increase in size and responsibility as Obamanians suggest? Or is something smaller, leaner a better solution?

Finding Just Right isn't an endpoint, it's a journey. Most assuredly our current metric for government consumption of our resources, that state, local and federal governments consumes 40% of our economy, with the federal government consuming about 24.1% and growing, is not a workable solution for any kind of greatness. This size translates into if 2% GDP growth and 7.7% unemployment and is well short of greatness.

What is great? Before we delve into three metrics that are seldom discussed by are crucial to our national greatness, here are four key indicators that are sometimes difficult to discover, even on the Internet, but with which most Americans should become familiar as the elements of our American scorecard.

Real Gross Domestic Product Growth. The GDP growth number generally reported is actually Nominal GDP. This number is the difference between last year's GDP, say $10 trillion, and the current year, say $11 trillion, or 10% GDP growth. This number, however, contains inflation, and if inflation increased 11%, then negative growth of 1% occurred. Not so good for the average

American. So Real GDP growth is the key indicator. Great Real GDP growth, an A, should be graded as anything above 3.5% and below 6% (too much growth can drive inflation.) From 2.5% to 3.5% is a B. From 1.5% to 2.5% a C. From 0% to 2% a D. Failing is obvious. Real GDP growth during the five-year stretch for the Obama administration is just below zero, nominal GDP averaged just over 2%.

Unemployment Rate and Labor Participation Rate: These two indicators are linked and, together, provide a great picture of employment health than just the unemployment rate which is published monthly in the press. A low unemployment rate with a high participation rate translates into a very healthy economy. The government actually measures a vast array of variables but generally the only statistic reported is the unemployment rate. The Labor Participation rate provides better insight about how many people may have left the labor market as they have given up actively seeking employment. Great rates, an A, translate to: Unemployment: Below 4.25%, Participation: Over 67%. For a B: 4.25% to 5%, and 66% to 67%. For a C, 5% to 6% and 65% to 66%. A grade of D is earned for 6% to 7% and 64% to 65%. Above these rates is failure. Today's rates are 7.3% and 63.2%, indicative of a poor economy.

Gross Capital Investment/GDP Rate: Tracking this percentage over the last several decades, this rate rises and falls with overall economic activity. When it is down, the economy suffers. When it is high, the economy excels.   When the rate is over 20%, the economic on A track.   Anything below this rate should be understood as a warning signal. (International Monetary Fund, 2013) Clinton's and Reagan's years of strong growth had rates of 20 percent or more. Obama's rates have ranged from 14% to 17%.

Percent of Population Obtaining Federal Assistance: Great social programs work so well, fewer and fewer citizens require assistance. American Leftists track the opposite metrics as a standard bearer of enlightened social policy: the number of people getting public assistance. Though this is a bit counter-intuitive, the marketing is well done and the result is it feels like the government is a good and charitable Samaritan. The reality is quite the opposite. If more and more citizens need help then the government hasn't created an healthy economy for job creation and/or hasn't educated our children well enough to be able to find a job if there were one to be had. The greatest nation with the most enlightened social policy will have few if any citizens on the public dole. Currently, our government is sending in excess of 80,000,000 transfer payments, otherwise known as redistribution of wealth, to American citizens, around 25% of the population. If 0% is an A+, then 25% is surely an F.

But these metrics are for the citizen to monitor the quality of governance. What are the key indicators the government also needs to track to assure American excellence beyond the basics above?

Measuring Government Success: What Is Just Right?

There is a sweet spot for Just Right. Goldilocks found hers at the Three Bears house: twice! Good eats and a good bed. Just Right has a strike zone. The strike zone is refined. It has edges that, when missed, are simply Balls. There is plenty of room outside the strike zone, abundant room. Wild pitches wind up in the dirt or occasionally the stands. Throw enough balls, and you walk in the winning runs for the other team. Not good. Throw strikes and you have a chance to win. Goldilocks threw two strikes: the right porridge and the right bed. She threw one really bad ball, one that was way out of the strike zone. She wasn't in her own home. In general, it's not a good idea to appropriate other people's (bear's) property. So, as bears tend to eat more than porridge, Goldi was smart to leave. Maybe her exit is a strike as well.

One might think that Goldilocks' decision to eat baby bear's porridge and sleep in his bed were Just Right that the direction of this book is toward little or no government. Not really. The Colonies tried to band together creating a very small government in the form of the Articles of Confederation and it did not work. The Articles were out of the strike zone. Too little government creates its own set of problems: no superstructure to create a civil society or a strong union of states. Add no mechanism to lay or collect taxes so America could fund a very big war against the British and a government too small becomes less than Just Right. The government of the very least, did not, a great nation make. The founding fathers knew that though government was the enemy of liberty, *that both too little was problematic as well as too much!*

However, using Constitutional limits of power as a guide to sizing government, including the lack of success of government monopolies as a sidebar, then using transformational solutions suggested earlier in this section would leave the federal government at about 45% of the current budget or $1.764 trillion. With an estimated $16 trillion GDP for 2013, a transformed government would consume 11% of our economy, a far cry from today's 24.1%. This transformation is possible with better governance, but the transformation could not occur overnight. But transforming even one-half of the $2.04 trillion spent on Social Security, Medicare, Medicaid, Education, and Highways would result in millions of new jobs created, millions of jobs the lower quadrant of our society desperately needs to get on their individual roads to success. *Just Right for government should likely be in the 11% range, give or take a few percent.*

Is a government that consumes 11% of GDP the perfect size? Not necessarily. Government size will vary with stretches of high economic productivity, wars, and those times when Congress takes its eyes off the budget ball.

Although the size of government is a key metric for understanding the efficiencies of a nation, it is not the only key indicator. Key Process Indicators for social policy must be tied to the greatness of the nation based on those variables that create and sustain social, economic and cultural greatness.

I propose three key indicators and that great governance should pay great attention to. One indicator is economic, one social and on cultural. When these indicators are working at optimal levels and government size stays inside an 11% sweet spot, then the long-term sustainability of American greatness is assured:

- Innovation
- Family creation and permanence
- Educational Achievement

More than a few economists may read these three indicators and convulse. What about GDP? What about employment and inflation? And I couldn't agree more. They are indeed part of the American economic scorecard above. And there are numerous economic indicators that are key metrics that should be measured and evaluated. But these three measurements are core indicators of the health, not just of our economy bet the wellness of our society and culture. Greatness cannot be achieved if these KPIs begin to whither. As these go, so goes our country.

Innovation

Innovation is directly connected to the success of an economy. Our national economy is directly coupled with its ability to attract the best innovators and coupled to a high propensity to adopt their innovations. Innovation drives several important economic metrics including, economic growth, employment, and productivity.

As one might imagine, when innovation is high, productivity will likely increase, increasing employment, which increases family creation and permanence, which creates upward pressure on the need for a better education. As noted early, Joyce Appleby cited innovation as a key barometer for capitalism's success. Ms. Appleby is most certainly correct. During the industrial revolution, English success could easily be traced by the adoption of steam engines as a source of industrial power generation. Because England had nearly twice the steam engines as its nearby competitors in Europe, national output grew rapidly. Wealth grew. Pay for laborers was the highest in Europe. Capitalism flourished.

Steam engines were first in a long line of energy solutions that helped propel economies throughout the world. America has been innovation central for two centuries. Our preeminence in innovation creation has driven economic excellence with a cornucopia of inventions from the cotton gin, telegraph, telephone, personal computer and the internet. Even the iPad changed the fashion we consume and use information from songs for kids, to interactive, dashboarding for executives to monitor the health of their business.

Three key metrics to measure for innovation success are:
- Immigration policy that focuses on attracting the best and brightest researchers, technical entrepreneurs, science students seeking degrees and advanced degrees from our universities, and policies that lead to citizenship for these categories
- Continual improvement in the Economic Freedom Index (transparency, ease of setting up and conducting business, among others)
- Continuing emphasis in our university system as technology and research incubators

Our immigration policy has flunked its mission. Not only has the federal government incomprehensibly ignored its responsibilities to protect our borders, is has allow any foreign national to make a unilateral immigration choice, outside immigration law, walking across the border to get a job. While millions simply walk across the border, the government's most important mission, to bring the best and brightest to America and assure their continued presence either as entrepreneurs or high-skilled workers with permanent residence has actually worsened. Many who have completed their education are sent home as no green cards are available for these important economic producers. Worse entrepreneurs trying to get to America to set up business, have no access due to the very limited supply of green cards. Poor immigration policy is driving a new generation of innovators to other parts of the world, especially Asia. Because of poor domestic immigration policy and improved economic conditions in China and India, a steady supply of researchers and students from these countries is diminishing.

The Kaufman index of entrepreneurial activity may be a useful, non-government index as it measures immigrant and naturalized citizen business creation. This very important metric shows that 'Immigrants were more than twice as likely as were the native-born to start businesses each month in 2011.' (Fairlee, 2012) The report noted that who account for 12.9 percent of the population, started 28 percent of all new U.S. businesses in 2011. When immigration policy focuses on bringing the best and brightest immigrants to the U.S., when government seeks to maximize the immigration benefit by assuring technical entrepreneurs are an important part of the mix, then immigration's economic impact will be maximized. Not every business will produce an innovation that changes the world like TV or radio or the telephone. The chances, though, for that great, new innovation being American, increase if America is the largest repository of innovators and business people.

Increased emphasis for technical and science émigrés simply adds to our limited set of homegrown researchers, innovators and technical business creators. The result is an increased pool of investment capital seeking new products to support, more jobs, and, potential with new inventions, higher productivity.

Coupled tightly to immigration policy, our economic freedom is essential not only to us, the current residents; but to immigrants as great economic freedom is a magnet for ideas and investment. Although there is more than one organization that has developed economic freedom indexes, the Heritage Foundations may be the most well knows. Ten economic freedoms are categorized broadly in four areas:

- Rule of Law (property rights, freedom from corruption);
- Limited Government (fiscal freedom, government spending);
- Regulatory Efficiency (business freedom, labor freedom, monetary freedom); and

- Open Markets (trade freedom, investment freedom, and financial freedom).

America's Freedom index dropped over the last five years from 80.9 and fifth freest nation in the world to 76 and 10th place. Next year with the advent of Obamacare and further implementation of Dodd-Frank and an increasingly intrusive EPA, our rating will continue to dissolve, harming our ability to attract émigrés, investment and increase our base of employment. Liberal governance and economics will lead America back up the road of Economic Freedom.

Education

Education is the crucial building block for building a great and enduring American society, culture and economy. A good society is possible with only a small percentage of society is educated. A great society is impossible to sustain unless nearly every single citizen is well-educated. Well-educated does not necessarily include a college education. In fact, a great education can be had from a very high quality high school education. Even a mediocre high school education would be a vast improvement for about half of American children. Perhaps as much as 25% of American children never drive onto the education on-ramp, receiving inadequate math and reading skills in elementary schools from their very first day of school. Without a high quality start in first grade, lack of reading skills will erode the ability to learn any subject. With marginal abilities in addition, subtraction, multiplication and division, higher level math becomes impossibility, science a vast wasteland. Middle school and high school engagement for civics and history becomes a blank page for the low achieving reader. Far too many students are unable to participate in our culture, including the American Economic Dream, because the tools they should have acquired in elementary schools weren't.

What is especially disconcerting is that this indictment is not new. Government education has had the same issues for 35 years, since the federal government decided to directly enter the monopoly for education. With district consolidations in the 1960's into local government monopolies, states followed with more regulation and control, the feds upped the ante with their involvement and unions added pressure for more pay and rules. The outcome? While educational achievement flat-lined spending doubled from 1970 to 2009 from $4596 to $10,694 in 2005 dollars according the National Center for Education Statistics. (National Center for Education Statistics, 2013) Worse, according to Lindsay Burke of the Heritage Foundation, the number of students in our schools has been relatively flat since 1970, up only 8% while the number of teachers has increased 60% and non-teaching staff a whopping 138%. (Burke, 2012) Yet, education output has really not improved much at all. ACTs and SATs are up a tiny increment. Most important, inner city education is still a train wreck. Voters should ask how funding could increase by a factor of two, teachers and staff nearly the same, and yet no meaningful improvement occur? The simple answer, money and teachers and staff are not at issue, as noted earlier in this section. Whatever solution is erected and tested, measuring results must take precedent, not what money is spent.

But what to measure? To make it simple, I believe there is a single metric that lead is leading education indicator of success, a 4th grade reading by National Assessment of Education Progress or NEAP. In 1970, 4th graders scored 212. Today, that score increased a whopping 8 points, 5 points appearing to come from a change in scoring methods in 2009. Regardless, a 4% increase in productivity is a poor payback for a 132% increase in spending. Those children, who do well on this test, tend to do better in school because the can read and comprehend their lessons.

Increasing the first through fourth grade reading scores, especially those in the large cities where scores in 2011 were 211, to a number in the range of what children in private schools obtain, 231, would significantly enhance graduation rates for those in the inner city for two reasons. First, this fourth grade reading schools is a primary indicator for gradation. If you can't read, you can't learn and at some point give up. Second, raising this rate will have a huge impact on several other metrics for social success including job acquisition, improved health and ultimately the expectation for marriage.

Additionally, this test should be performed in 1st, 2nd and 3rd grades. A child that isn't reading in the first couple of months in 1st grade is at risk or never learning to read well enough to do much of anything in life, and will most assuredly wind up in long line with other seeking any job, most likely a minimum wage job – for life.

Marriage

A society will not be long lived if marriage goes out of fashion as it has in America. In the early 1950's 96% of couples chose to marry. Today, the rate is only 60%. In many inner cities only 1 in 5 women choose to marry. In 1980, Charles Murray who described, in *Losing Ground*, how American welfare policies created a series of poor economic choices that drove potential marriage partners apart. Accepting government assistance, as non-married partner, proved more economical beneficial than getting married and working. More recently, in Murray's *Cultural Divide*, he showed the effect of these policies over the last thirty years not only harmed the lower quadrant economically but culturally, too.

The effect has been enormously destructive to those most in need, depriving them of a path to job, marriage, and even faith. His analysis is sad testimony to our poor federal governance. His insight is invaluable and is quoted as some length. Per Murray:

> 'When Americans used to brag about "the American way of life"—a phrase still in common use in 1960— they were talking about a civic culture that swept an extremely large proportion of Americans of all classes into its embrace. It was a culture encompassing shared experiences of daily life and shared assumptions about

American values involving marriage, honesty, hard work and religiosity.

Over the past 50 years, that common civic culture has unraveled. We have developed a new upper class with advanced educations, often obtained at elite schools, sharing tastes and preferences that set them apart from mainstream America. At the same time, we have developed a new lower class, characterized not by poverty but by withdrawal from America's core cultural institutions.' (Murray, 2012)

Murray outlines the growing cultural divisions in two specific geographies, Belmont and Fishtown. Belmont is upper crust and high income earners. Fishtown is blue collar, but its inhabitants have a high school education. He does not delve into the inner city and its metrics, but the differences in these two towns, one upper middle class, the other lower middle, is further indictment of how government attempts to engineer society then fails to measure the effects of its work.

Murray reviews marriage, single parentage, industriousness, crime and religiosity. What he found is that two towns were much alike in these metrics in the 1960s had largely diverged by 2010. Faith, family and hard work while remaining much the same in Belmont had flagged seriously in Fishtown. Murray continues:

'As I've argued in much of my previous work, I think that the reforms of the 1960s jump-started the deterioration. Changes in social policy during the 1960s made it economically more feasible to have a child without having a husband if you were a woman or to get along without a job if you were a man; safer to commit crimes without suffering consequences; and easier to let the government deal with problems in

186

your community that you and your neighbors formerly had to take care of.' (Murray 2012)

...

'The only thing that can make a difference is the recognition among Americans of all classes that a problem of cultural inequality exists and that something has to be done about it. That "something" has nothing to do with new government programs or regulations. Public policy has certainly affected the culture, unfortunately, but unintended consequences have been as grimly inevitable for conservative social engineering as for liberal social engineering.

The "something" that I have in mind has to be defined in terms of individual American families acting in their own interests and the interests of their children. Doing that in Fishtown requires support from outside. There remains a core of civic virtue and involvement in working-class America that could make headway against its problems if the people who are trying to do the right things get the reinforcement they need—not in the form of government assistance, but in validation of the values and standards they continue to uphold. The best thing that the new upper class can do to provide that reinforcement is to drop its condescending "nonjudgmentalism." Married, educated people who work hard and conscientiously raise their kids shouldn't hesitate to voice their disapproval of those who defy these norms. When it comes to marriage and the work ethic, the new upper class must start preaching what it practices.' (Murray, 2012)

In short, Murray is suggesting the federal government's central planning, not just regarding economics, but social welfare as well, is not effective and harms the very culture that drives American greatness. To restate Murray and a litany of other social scientists, the four key indicators of personal success are built on four cultural metrics: family, education, hard work and faith, family being the key indicator of how well the other three are engaged.

To be a great nation, our current rate of single parentage at 40% is simply unacceptably high. America needs to move the marriage needle north of 95% to approach greatness, to assure the health of our future civil society's health. To maximize our greatness, a score of 95% or above is required. And Murray's advice is correct; no amount of central planning from the Left or Right is going to help. What is important is that neither the government nor its citizens should condone poor conduct, whether that is single parentage, poor educational achievement, or irresponsible criminal activity.

LIBERTY'S INTANGIBLES

What have Dreams and Cowboys and Magic to do with one another? With Freedom? Everything. The result of the culture of liberty, the empowered citizen, isn't simply that America is able to grow an economy second to none. Great economics are wonderful, but the subtle results, the ones that are not so obvious and are seldom measured much less noticed may be the most important results of all. And that's why it is important to key our eyes on Mickey and Paula the Great and that cowboy you will never meet but should probably honor.

The Next Frontier

American exceptionalism has produced a steady stream of comments from friends and foes around the world, beginning with the mocking of our Great Experiment by European nobility in the late 1700s. The original non-internet blogger, Alexis deTocqueville, wrote about America's new society, a frontier society with limitless ability to expand on the continent. Though our democracy was not perfect it did perform in a way that produced good effects for the many. In Tocquellville's words:

> 'When the rich alone govern, the interest of the poor is always endangered; and when the poor make the laws, that of the rich incurs very serious risks. The advantage of democracy does not consist, therefore, as has sometimes been asserted, in favoring the prosperity of all, but simply in contributing to the well-being of the greatest possible number.' (Tocqueville, 2012)

The poor farmer had the same opportunity owned by a rich kid. A young man like Benjamin Franklin, one of 17 children born to a poor candle maker had the same chance for success as Thomas Jefferson whose father was a planter and surveyor.

The tone of *Democracy in America* is both at once amazed that democracy worked so well despite the disadvantages of distributing power to states, localities and individuals; and laudatory because it worked so well, for so many. Certainly, the political efforts in our democracy have been to attempt to create the best possible environment for everyone's success. The HOW of our methods is seldom perfect and certainly our current political endeavors to perfect society have lacked even mediocre results, but the intent, regardless of political party has been genuine.

As we have veered off course, away from the tutelage of the founding fathers, it is occasionally important to hear what the competition is saying about America. There are the naysayers from the former Hugo Chavez and the unintelligible rants of North Korea's Kim Jong Eun, but not all comments from the international community are political cantering and propaganda. Former Singapore Prime Minister Lee Kuan Yew recently had much to say on the topic of American exceptionalism in his book, *A Statemen's Friendly Advice.* Peggy Noonan reviewed the book in the Wall Street Journal. Yew makes several valuable insights.

> 'The American advantage in coming economic and technological contest? A "can-do" approach to life. Americans always believe a problem can be solver. An "entrepreneurial culture' that sees both risk and failure " as natural and necessary for success.'
>
> ...
>
> The U.S. is still "a frontier society." "The American culture...is that we start from scratch and beat you." They would settle and empty area, call it a town, and say, "You be the sheriff, I am the judge, you are the policeman, and you are the banker, let us start." Not long ago the U.S. was losing to Japan and Germany in manufacturing. "But {Americans} came with the Internet, Microsoft and Bill Gates, and Dell ....What kind of mindset do you need for that? It is part of their

history.'

...

'And America goes the way of modern Europe at its peril: "If you follow the ideological direction of Europe, you are done for." There are always people who require help, but "addressing their needs must be done in a way that does not kill incentive."' (Noonan, 2012)

That frontier, can-do attitude, doesn't arrive at our doorstep one Saturday morning in the form of a Fed in a three-piece suite saying, "Hi, I'm Joe. I'm here from the Federal Government. I am here to help you create that can-do attitude." That attitude is a result of the culture of liberty, of the empowered citizen. Government doesn't tell you to get another job or a new job when you need money or more money to pay your bills. Government doesn't say, 'Mr. Edison, I think it will take at least 2000 tries to make the light bulb idea work.' No one was in the garage with Jobs or Wozniak to help put together the first Apple computer. And most certainly no one told the poor, English immigrant to get on a boat and come to America to get a piece of land he could own and farm. No one comes to this country or no one in this country listens to the government as its inspiration to create, to work, to consider, to dream, to do anything. The buck stops with each of us. And guess what; most every American is just fine with possessing his or her own dreams.

After nearly two and a half centuries we are still a Frontier Society with a Can Do attitude, and thank God we are. Today's frontiers aren't little dusty towns like 19th century Tombstone, Arizona. Today's frontiers are the human genome, space travel, and String Theory.

If anyone, anywhere in the world wants to challenge the next frontier, America is the best game in town because everyone is free to pursue their dreams. Poor or rich. Educated or uneducated. Only the motivated need apply.

Faith; Tradition and a Wide Grin.

I cannot help but smile at weddings, graduations, and baptisms.

Weddings paint wide smiles, but also produce moments of great solemnity and tears of joy. For those who chose a civil path to marriage, you will miss the emotional power of a church wedding. It is huge opportunity lost. The marriage ceremony is not just for the bride and groom but the congregation as well. This event isn't for the faint of heart seeking a relationship for physical rapture and sharing rent.

Marriage is a life-long covenant which translates into 'until death do us part.'

Marriage is also a beautiful moment captured sometimes in church, sometimes in a more secure but lovely location, still hosted by a pastor and his Godly invocations. The joy of a mother and father watching the entrance of their daughter, the bride, brings boundless joy to all who attend. It is hard to imagine, that at any wedding, this moment does not bring a smile to every single person.

A sermon about love, about the commitment of marriage, and of God's blessings and sacrament of marriage enjoins everyone present with a responsibility to the long term health and seriousness of the commitment to marriage. And the vows should make any man and woman takes a giant emotional gulp, a gut check, because the vows are forever. Marriage is that important as a commitment to each other, and as a commitment to producing the next generation of humanity. Marriage is not a part time job. It is hard work. It is not about what you get from marriage, but what you give, and when given, whatever gift that may be, the return is always multiplied.

'Love is patient and kind; love does not envy or boast;
it is not arrogant or rude. It does not insist on its own
way; it is not irritable or resentful; it does not rejoice at
wrongdoing, but rejoices with the truth. Love bears all

things, believes all things, hopes all things, and endures all things. Love never ends. As for prophecies, they will pass away; as for tongues, they will cease; as for knowledge, it will pass away. For we know in part and we prophesy in part, but when the perfect comes, the partial will pass away. When I was a child, I spoke like a child; I thought like a child, I reasoned like a child. When I became a man, I gave up childish ways. For now we see in a mirror dimly, but then face to face. Now I know in part; then I shall know fully, even as I have been fully known. So now faith, hope, and love abide, these three; but the greatest of these is love.' (Bible, 13:4-13)

Finding wisdom is not an easy task if government finds it necessary to rip our traditions from our lives. The Left has spent much effort nipping seditiously at the edges of the hallowed tradition of marriage, and its supporting foundation, religion. Reducing the value of marriage ultimately harms the notion of love itself and debilitates society's most fundamental emotion and economic unit, the family.

The intangible value of a religious marriage that endures is that permanence creates the strongest possible foundation for the pursuit of happiness. Though great economic benefit results from marriage, the real lasting benefit is the broad grin of the bride, the groom and the congregation during the wedding and the warm smile of giving that paints a lifetime of happiness produced by a marriage that endures. The challenges and fights and difficulties of any relationship are supplanted by the understanding that in partnership, one does not have to go it alone.

Cowboys, Farmers...and other institutions of hard work

In the ramp up to the War in Iraq, the Left called George Bush a *cowboy!* For the Left, calling the enemy a Cowboy is an insult of the greatest potential. As most Leftists, actually as most Americans, have never met a cowboy, they would be astonished to discover, that cowboys are not gunslingers ready pull their six-shooters for a gun fight, but are Great Americans who value hard work, the hardest work imaginable, their family, and personal responsibility. Many of these traits common to the American cowboy are extended their brethren ranchers and farmers. Cowboys, a group that is sadly dwindling, are important examples of America's rugged individualism, and the best of what America offers to the world. During SuperBowl LXVII, Dodge Corporation produced a wonderful commercial honoring toughness, honoring farmers and indirectly, cowboys and ranchers and every hardworking American that ever lived. Paul Harvey, who died in 2009, narrated. Here are a few excerpts:

> 'God said I need somebody willing to get up before dawn, milk the cows, work all day in the field, milk cows again, eat supper then go to town and stay past midnight at a meeting of the school board – So God made a Farmer
>
> God said I need somebody willing to sit up all night with and newborn colt, and watch it die, then dry his eyes and say maybe next year. I need somebody who can shape an axe handle from a persimmon sprout, shoe a horse with a hunk of car tire, who can make a harness out of hay wire, feed sacks and shoe straps, who at planting time and harvest season will finish his forty hour week by Tuesday noon and then, paining from tractor back, will put in another 72 hours – So God made a Farmer.

Somebody who would bale a family together with the soft, strong bonds of sharing; who would laugh and then sigh, and then reply with smiling eyes when his son says he wants to spend his life doing what dad does – So God made a Farmer.' (Harvey, 2013)

As so too did God make Cowboys and every hardworking American throughout its history.

Cowboys and their compatriots in hard work, character, integrity and a litany of other personal measures of success, are the very incarnation of American greatness. Mocking the institution by naming George Bush to this great club shows the shallowness of the Left and their blithe arrogance about what should be revered by us all. Knowing and hoping there will always be a contingent of cowboys in our society is incredibility important. To lose this mini-culture of hard work and toughness is to diminish America.

Paula the Great

When most of us think of great persons, we think of presidents and generals and titans of industry or science. Sports figures that burst records are heroes for many of our youth. It is not unreasonable to think of Lincoln or Patton or Carnegie or Einstein or Jeter and know that these Americans were indeed great. But they were not the cornerstone of building a great society. They are a part of history but only a small part of our daily quest toward greatness.

When we think of great, we should think of Paula. Paula is the cornerstone of our great society, as are millions of other mothers, who, generation after generation, replenish our society one child at a time. Like every mom in America, Paula had the great fortune of living in a country in which our social contract, our constitution, provided the liberty for everyone to achieve their own level of greatness. Though we all have much in common, each of our paths have slightly different courses which are important and, when taking a minute of recollect a long string of one's history, the challenges and successes, are all inevitably delicious. As is Paula's.

Paula had a bit of the frontier women in her, in part because Paula was born on the Indian reservation in Northern Arizona, but also because she was granddaughter of Sedona Schnebly, the namesake of Sedona, Arizona. Sedona was very much a frontier woman. The city had only 20 families in 1902 when T.C., Sedona's husband and new postmaster, put her name on postal stamp because the government felt the other potential names like Oak Creek Canyon were too long.

Paula has some of the toughness of a frontier settler that is complemented by her common sense and a no poppycock attitude about life. She is also kind, gentle, loving a wife of 55 years, and the mother of three. She is durable because her character and faith were strong. She is charitable and knew better than the rest of us that it isn't what you receive in life that makes life great, it is what you give. And though these are important traits and what makes her a good woman, what makes her great is the legacy she will leave America – another generation of Paula's.

Her three daughters all have the delightful combination of mental toughness and endurance mixed with faith and charity, and they are building what Paula built, a new generation of Americans that are a little smarter, a bit more charitable, perhaps even a bit wiser, though exceeding the wisdom of Paula will take many more years of experience that comes with age. What makes Paula remarkable is that her strength of character is well and alive in her grandchildren as well. It is remarkable that so much of Paula shows up in her daughters *and* their children. Such force of will is not common and very welcome in an age where each of the last few generations have lost many of the traits of previous generations, like the importance of family or requirement for hard work. For Paula's progeny these are stronger.

Every generation produces a small army of Paula the Greats. When there are fewer rather than more Paula's, which has been something that has been a trend for a generation or two, America is less well off. We need more Paula's. We need lots more Paula's to assure the super-structure of our great nation remains strong and vibrant. If Paul Harvey were still alive he might narrate an ode about how the hard work of Mom's – 'And so God made Paula.'

Great leaders will come and go, but Paula the Great and her army of moms are forever.

Magic, Mickey, and the Art of the Possible

Progressivism, communism, fascism, socialism, totalitarianism, statism, any and all philosophies of the left... they all have one fatal error – none of them had or have Mickey Mouse. In fact, it is highly unlikely that any 'ism' could have ever conceived the notion of Mickey. The 'isms were Mickeyless, and the ideologies doomed to failure because of it.

I used to believe that America's great political and economic experiments were only a result of hope derived from economic and political freedom. The Revolution and the Constitution were the foundation for the construction of extraordinary country where hope reigned in every hard working heart. But there is something more to America's Great Experiment. If hope is the heart of the success, then Mickey and magic are the blood that nourishes our beliefs, ideas, and lives. Hope is built from family and friends and churches and schools .... from our culture and especially our culture of liberty. Magic, though, allows us the freedom to believe in things that may not otherwise be reasonable but are nevertheless very special, like God and Love and Mickey and his magical friends.

I wasn't much of a Mickey fan until I went to Disneyworld and Mickey's Magic Kingdom with my children. Living inside the gates of Disneyland for a few days assured me without any question the Mickey factor for building great cultures cannot be ignored. If there is a precursor to hope, it is the magic of Mickey. There is an ocean of magic in Mickey. He is not only a wonderful image for a young child's mind. He is the fulcrum of economic success for a man named Walt who had a dream. When it is possible for Walt to lay thinking before bedtime and imagine that 'a happy mouse with a goofy grin may just be the ticket to success,' well, that is the Mickey factor? When a little two-year-old looks up at Mickey and cannot help but smile and reach out for a hug that, too, is the Mickey factor. And after fifty years and a lot of different Disney characters, Walt thrived because millions of little kids and little kids' parents soak up a little of that magic every year.

Mickey could not have been invented elsewhere in the world. Had Walt grown up in North Korea or China or the Soviet Union or even Hitler's Germany for that matter, Mickey would have been a dream with no outlet. Perhaps after another few decades of 'openness' in Asia, freedom will reign and minds will open to such silly but wonderful possibilities. Perhaps. Perhaps, not. Europe may someday again find the special and energetic intellectual freedom of the Renaissance, but until then the mantle of socialism and corrosive nature of political correctness Mickey will be kept at bay. Even Mickey as an immigrant, an American import to France, has not done very well.

Mickey is special, an American special. He is not simply a product. He is magic. He is wonder in a child's eye, and wonder and love reflected in his parent's eye. He is also a business, a thriving, vibrant business. The success of that business is built on the foundation of hope resting on the expectation that the world is, after all, a good and moral place. Why? Because, at least in America, there is a little Mickey in all of us, or at least a desire to have a bit of Mickey on our team. Let's face it. He's a good guy that plays by the rules. There is much to love in that notion. Mickey reminds us that for all the bad we read in the paper every day there is monumental cascade of people creating a little magic of their own, working behind the scenes helping their fellow man.

And to the 'isms, including America's Left which has lost touch with America's founding roots as well as the magic in Mickey, the world must look pretty bleak. There is no chance in hell that friends of Saddam or the mullahs in Iran, or Robert Mugabe, or Herbert Croly his progeny of Progressives, or any despot could found a government that produces the individual freedom that could generate such a wild and crazy idea like the magic of Mickey. For the poor souls who lost their lives in Taliban controlled Afghanistan, hope and magic were simply beat into submission.

The founding fathers had no idea Mickey would arrive one day, but their courage to believe in the Great Experiment, that individuals free to pursue and publish ideas, no matter how outrageous, means Mickey could exist and thrive. In a marketplace of ideas, the good and great succeed and the bad and awful flounder and die. Perhaps America, and only America, where the marketplace is wildly open, and where everyday 300,000,000 Americans vote for what succeeds and what does not, is the last and best hope for Mickey and Sleepy and Snow White and so many others.

The day we left Disneyland I was left with the memory of Walt sitting in his den thinking about the genesis of Mickey and his magic kingdom and the hard work to take a crazy idea to a share dream for so many children. As for the Left who exterminates and controls ideas not of their creation, a culture without Mickey is a culture doomed to the ash heap of history. Mickey's magic is worth fighting for, just like the freedom that created the foundation which allowed Disney to create an industry as silly as a mouse with a goofy smile and a heart of gold. God Bless Mickey Mouse.

Conclusions

For the Left, they have a plan for you, the General Will as touted by a litany of social experiments and controls of national destiny. It is a plan where power is centralized in a few to the exclusion of the many. God, too, has a plan. God has given the power to us in the form of free will. Our destiny is ours. The choice of how we use God's gifts is ours. God is a Liberal God as he gives us the freedom to succeed with the cornucopia of gifts he has given us, or to fail. Our liberties are given by Him and by Nature. Great governments, Liberal Governments, are formed to protect the rights of their citizens. Leftist governments arrogantly assume that they both 'giveth rights and taketh them away.'

God is not only the God of Love, but also of art and of science. God is the penultimate leader in that he knows that our freedom allows us to achieve the greatest heights: morally, socially, economically and in all things. God did not create a determined universe to micro-manage. He allows us to freely choose between a Leftist, micro-managed world where our freedoms are not ours, or a universe where we are free to choose between right and wrong, good and bad.

I don't believe in determinism. I do believe God is great at everything. Science, love, forgiveness, and leadership. But I believe the greatest gift God gave us is Free Will because the giving of power and responsibilities is what great leaders do by nature. And God is the greatest leader. As in a Liberal Democracy, the rulebook is simple, not complicated and confusing. God gave us only ten rules to live by, not 20 or 50, or 2000 pages of exhaustive rules. Thankfully, Moses did not have to tote down a cartful of tablets from Mount Sinai. Our gifts are great, but our mission simple. Do what God, and what most all of us know is right and good, or don't, then face the consequences.

Greatness is possible because of the gifts given by God which we choose to use and the freedoms provided by God and Nature. Liberal government should never diminish or append these rights. The job of government is to protect our rights. The Founding Fathers had an appreciation of the American cultural and wove the culture threads of faith and reason, decentralized power, individual, and the American ethic for hard work into a Constitution and Bill of Rights the created our Foundation for Liberal Governance.

Peers and prognosticators of their time called our early nationhood and these new rules of governance, the Great Experiment. It was a great experiment. It is still a great experiment, one that has also sadly introduced a cascade of leftist experiments that ran counter to our Liberal traditions and have taken American down a road of mediocre results. As Charles Murray suggests: 'America is coming apart. For most of our nation's history, whatever the inequality in wealth between the richest and poorest citizens, we maintained a cultural equality known nowhere else in the world...' Tocqueville had clearer insight about the cohesive nature of 19th American civil society.

> 'The more opulent citizens take great care not to stand aloof from the people," wrote Alexis de Tocqueville, the great chronicler of American democracy, in the 1830s. "On the contrary, they constantly keep on easy terms with the lower classes: They listen to them, they speak to them every day.' (deTocqueville, 2013)

The notions of the Left, of Progressives, and Statists, of the intellectual and political elites, have betrayed not just our strong economic foundations built on personal liberty and free markets, but have also created poorly conceived social welfare policies which have built a new, permanent underclass, now 80 million citizens and growing.

This is no surprise to many Americans as the roots of our dispute about social welfare have origins centuries old. In the 19th century, David Ricardo lamented that even the meager Poor Laws of England in the 18th Century were designed not to make 'the poor, rich, but to make for the rich and the poor poorer.' Great social policy understands that money is not the core problem with poverty. Lack of money is a symptom. The core issues, especially today, are cultural and have more to do with lack of family formation, education, and skills development. Poor Leftist economic policy has exacerbated personal wealth grow, decapitating job growth with high borrowing and burdensome regulatory environments that cripple the abilities of businesses to grow and create jobs.

We are in a perfect storm of poor governance caused by central planning, economic justice, and a diminution of our liberties.

There is a path to success. That path will not be found in Washington, but there is a way out.

THE CHALLENGE

The 2012 federal elections were a surprise not just in the fact that, considering the dire position of our economy, Obama won, but that for well over a year, with both parties compiling a war chests totaling $1 billion each, that not one big idea was discussed, offered, debated, negotiated or advertised. Largely, $1 billion was spent on ideas that danced at the edges of our titanic problems, or worse, a wave of name-calling and bandwagoning. No candidate presented a plan to excise us from our giant mountain of debt or unfunded mandates for Social Security or Medicare; no one had a word to say about the sad condition of political leadership; and not one word about our debilitated culture of governance was uttered. Nothing. A year of nothing.

The election was a reallllly long Jerry Seinfeld episode, that delightfully hilarious sitcom about nothing. A half a billion dollars was spent by each party to assure their own little pond was undisturbed, that the status quo was held in check. One side nipped at the rich and paying their fair share of taxes. The other side quietly responded that we spend too much. No specifics, no plan, nothing strategic, nothing big, nothing that placed America back on the road to greatness.

This could have been Jerry Seinfeld's best show, biggest production, the longest show ever about nothing. And after the election, just to prove that the status quo was what each party was after, the 2012 Financial Cliff negotiations came to nothing. New taxes were implemented, a wishful $80 billion in new taxes on the rich, which by any estimation will likely total more like $40 billion or less in 2013, after many rich folks will do what rich folks always do when higher taxes are threatened, they will move their money elsewhere.

Two billion dollars spent for the 2012 election, in one year, and a lot of nothing. There are 537 (please exclude Paul Ryan who actually has a plan of sorts) elected federal politicians and not one has a solution to our problem. There are two parties that raise money to assure that two groups get their free tickets in this American Economy, either the social program recipient waiting for the federal debit card or the crony capitalist waiting for their tax exclusion or tax preference. Everyone wants their free ride. Big dollars are given to assure their free ride, and no one is representing the Average Joe like you and me. We pay our taxes, work hard, and try to get by, without representation.

Perhaps Liberalism will make a comeback in one party or another. You or I could run, tout Liberalism's extraordinary value and accomplishments. We could turn a party around, start a Liberal Revolution like Thomas Paine and 'Common Sense' during pre-revolutionary America. But seriously, one person, even armed with a good war chest in one federal district, one person among few hundred politicians whose funding comes from those protecting the status quo. That voice will either not be heard or significantly quieted by the cumulative war chests of both parties.

Key Principles: The Liberal Party of America

As there are no Liberals in Washington, the Liberal Party might be a good place to start.

I propose that this party be formed in a single Congressional District. Its founding principles are five:

- That liberty is the catalyst of greatness and that our liberties are given by God or from nature.
- That government is the enemy of liberty, whether too much or too little, and it is the job over government to assure neither too much or too little government exists, that finding Just Right is its primary mission.
- That a free nation does prosper and that a strong military is required to protect freedom from our enemies.

- That market solutions are the primary foundation of a successful economy and successful social policy.
- As power is the primary corrupter of all things, and money is power, the Liberal Party will optimize the power of the Average Joe by taking donations no higher than $195 per person or organization - whether Union, Business, individual voters, PACs, or 503Cs...$195.

The brand Liberal has been chosen for two reasons: 1) the policies and notions in this book and the principles on this page are Liberal notions, and 2) for far too long the Left has desecrated the Liberal Brand by obfuscating its true meaning and misrepresenting Leftist notions as Liberalism.

Even Republicans who regularly tout liberal themes as their own, mislabel Democrats as Liberal. But is it time for Americans to win back this brand. The word is now tarnished and meaningless and needs the rehabilitation it so richly deserves.

Should a new Liberal Party be formed, the Left will bring the full force of Big Brother; War is Peace, Freedom is Slavery, Ignorance is Strength, and Leftist is Liberal. Oh, how they will howl. Should this brand be reconstituted, Liberalism does have a chance to defeat the tired, staid, tepid ideas of both parties.

BIBLIOGRAPHY

Ahmari, S. (2013, September 1). *online.wsj.com.* Retrieved September 15, 2013, from Wall Street Joiurnal: online.wsj.com/.../SB10001424127887324108204579023143 97440842...

Air War College. (2013, August 4). The Nature of Command and Control. Australia.

Appelby, J. (2010). *The Relentless Revolution.* New York: W.W. Norton.

Arnold Harberger. (2009). *Monopoly and Resource Allocation, p. 84-6.* CPI Journal, Volume 5.

Barger, M. (1984, April 1). *What Killed Ma Bell?* Retrieved January 8, 2013, from The Freeman: http://www.fee.org/the_freeman/detail/what-killed-ma-bell#axzz2avDl0cEM

Beauty Schools Directory. (2012, December 27). *Arizona Board of Cosmetology Requirements.* Retrieved October 4, 2013, from Beauty Schools Directory: http://www.beautyschoolsdirectory.com/faq/license_az.php

Bible, T. (13:4-13). *The Bible.* King James Edition.

Bingham, A. (2012, September 18). *Mitt Romney's 47 Percent: Who Does Not Pay Incomes Taxes.* Retrieved May 17, 2013, from www.abcnews.com: http://abcnews.go.com/Politics/OTUS/mitt-romneys-47-percent-pay-income-taxes/story?id=17263629

Blum, J. M. (1970, p. 256). *Roosevelt and Morgenthau.* Boston: Houghton Mifflin Harcourt.

Brooks, A. (2012, May 8). *America and The Value of Earned Success.* Retrieved Februsry 12, 2013, from Wall Street Journal: http://online.wsj.com/article/SB1000142405270230474990457 7385650652966894.html

Buchanan, J. (1999). *Public Principles of Public Debt.* Indianaapolis: Liberty Fund.

Buchanan, J. (2003, Spring). Public Choice: Politics Without Romance. *The Quarterly Review of The Centre for Independent Studies*, 4.

Buchanan, J. (Spring 2003). Politics Without Romance. *The Quarterly Review of The Centre for Independent Studies*, p. 2.

Burke, L. (2012, October 15). *How Escalating Education Spending is Killing Crucial Reform.* Retrieved June 2, 2013, from Heritage Foundation: http://www.heritage.org/research/reports/2012/10/how-escalating-education-spending-is-killing-crucial-reform

Carmen Reinhard, K. R. (2010, January). *Growth in a Time of Debt.* Retrieved April 29, 2013, from NBER: http://www.nber.org/papers/w15639

Centers for Disease Control. (2007, p. 41). *CDC, Health, United States.* Retrieved May 10, 2013, from Centers for Disease Control: http://www.cdc.gov/nchs/data/hus/hus07.pdf

Charles de Secondat, B. d. (2011, Locations 1189-1191). *Montesquieu.* Kindle Edition.

Cheney, D. (2013, September 11). *Dick Cheney on the Budget & Economy.* Retrieved September 11, 2013, from On The Issues: http://www.ontheissues.org/2004/Dick_Cheney_Budget_+_Ec onomy.htm

Clark, S. J. (1953). *Atlantic*, 227.

Collins, J. (2001). *Good to Great.* New York: Harper Collins Pulbishers.

CRA International. (2006, Spring). *Sarbanes-Oxley Section 404 Costs and Implementation Issues.* Retrieved March 20, 2013, from CRA International: http://www.s-oxinternalcontrolinfo.com/pdfs/CRA_III.pdf)

Cravens, G. (2007, 113-114). *Power to Save The World.* New York: Random House.

Croly, H. (1911, p. 418). *The Promise of American Life.* New York: The Macmillan Company.

deTocqueville, A. (2013). *Democracy in America.* Retrieved May 29, 2013, from Google Books: http://books.google.com/books?id=2jQePTbog5QC&pg=PA111&lpg=PA111&dq=The+more+opulent+citizens+take+great+care+not+to+stand+aloof+from+the+people&source=bl&ots=B3q41QMV6p&sig=nHrib2y0NuhcyyXljVgcf-s3MzU&hl=en&sa=X&ei=eJBYUfzaHenD0AG4l4HgDQ&sqi=2&ved=0CDUQ6

Dodd-Frank. (2010). Senate Banking Committee, BRIEF SUMMARY OF THE DODD-FRANK WALL STREET REFORM AND CONSUMER PROTECTION ACT. Washington D.C.: US Senate.

Dolan, E. (2012, September 20). *Next August Job Numbers are a Disappointment for Democrats.* Retrieved April 22, 2013, from EconoMonitor: http://www.economonitor.com/dolanecon/2012/09/06/simplicity-vs-compexity-goodharts-law-and-the-financial-regulators-dilemma/

EPA. (2013, April 13). *Standards of Perfomance for Greenhous Gas Emissions from Stationary Sources.* Retrieved September 22, 2013, from EPA: http://www2.epa.gov/sites/production/files/2013-09/documents/20130920proposal.pdf

Etzkorn, A. S. (2013, March 29). *When Simplicity Is the Solution.* Retrieved March 29, 2013, from Wall Street Journal: http://online.wsj.com/article/SB1000142412788732400070457 8386652879032748.html?KEYWORDS=when+simplicity+is+th e+solution

Fairlee, R. W. (2012, March). *2011 Kauffman Index Of Entrepreneurial Activity.* Retrieved April 19, 2013, from Ewing Marion Kauffman Foundation: http://www.kauffman.org/uploadedFiles/KIEA_2012_report.pdf

Ferguson, A. (2013, May 6). *It Just Gets More and More Dismal.* Retrieved May 9, 2013, from Weekly Standard: http://www.weeklystandard.com/articles/it-just-gets-more-and-more-dismal_719171.html?page=2

Foley, E. (2013, May 15). *Obama Administration To Stop Deporting Younger Undocumented Immigrants and Grant Work Permits.* Retrieved September 28, 2013, from Huffington Post: http://www.huffingtonpost.com/2012/06/15/obama-immigration-order-deportation-dream-act_n_1599658.html

Fox News. (2013, September 30). *Obamacare 'glitch' watch: RI says state-run site still needs work.* Retrieved October 1, 2013, from Fox News: http://www.foxnews.com/politics/2013/09/30/obamacare-glitch-watch-delay-in-launch-spanish-language-sites/

Franklin, B. (1787, September 17). *Benjamin Franklin to the Federal Convention.* Retrieved December 28, 2012, from University of Chicago Press: http://press-pubs.uchicago.edu/founders/documents/a7s3.html

Goldberg, J. (2007). *Liberal Facism, Page 109.* New York: Doublday.

Gordon, R. J. (2012, December 22-23). *Why Innovation Won't Save Us.* Retrieved December 29, 2012, from Wall Street Journal: http://online.wsj.com/article/SB1000142412788732446160457 8191781756437940.html

Grund, D. H. (2013, March 23). *Networked Minds Require Fundamentally New Kind of Economics.* Retrieved March 23, 2013, from Science Daily: http://www.sciencedaily.com/releases/2013/03/130320115105.htm

Harvey, P. (2013, February 3). *Wow, Did that Dodge Ad with Paul Harvey Talking about Farmers Rock the Super Bowl.* Retrieved May 10, 2013, from The Blaze: http://www.theblaze.com/stories/2013/02/03/paul-harvey-talking-about-farmers-in-dodge-ad-wow-was-that-amazing/

Havighurst, C. (2002, October 2). How the Healthcare Revolution Fell Short. *Duke Law Scholarship Repository*, p. 24.

Hayek, L. V. (1944). *The Road to Serdom.* Chicago: Univerity of Chicago.

Health and Human Services. (2011, September). *Overview of the Uninsured in the United States: A Summary of the 2011 Current Population Survey.* Retrieved May 17, 2013, from Heatlth And Human Services: http://aspe.hhs.gov/health/reports/2011/cpshealthins2011/ib.shtml

Hurd, S. (2009, June 12). *How Safeway Is Cutting Health-Care Costs.* Retrieved May 24, 2013, from Wall Street Journal: http://online.wsj.com/article/SB124476804026308603.html

International Monetary Fund. (2013, October 13). *Find the Data.* Retrieved October 13, 2013, from World-economic-outlook,findthedata.com: http://world-economic-outlook.findthedata.org/l/5930/United-States

Investor's Daily. (2013, March 8). *Investor's Daily, More Are Quitting the Workforce Than Getting Jobs.* Retrieved March 8, 2013, from Investor's Daily: http://news.investors.com/ibd-editorials/030813-647381-job-growth-outpaced-by-growth-in-nonworkers.htm#ixzz2PyJSqUrB

Jefferson, T. (1743 – 1826). *The Writing of Thomas Jefferson, V. 8.*
Retrieved January 6, 2013, from Hathi Trust, Digital Library:
http://babel.hathitrust.org/cgi/pt?id=mdp.39015005705861;seq
=208#page/177/mode/1up

Johnson, L. B. (1965, July 1965). *President Lyndon B. Johnson's
remarks with President Truman at the signing in Independence
of the Medicare bill.* Retrieved May 2, 2013, from Lyndon
Baines Johnson Library:
http://www.lbjlib.utexas.edu/johnson/archives.hom/speeches.h
om/650730.asp

Keynes, M. (1920-2, Pages 285-7). *Collected Writings Volume 17.*
Cambridge: Cambridge University Press.

Keynes, M. (1926). *End of Laissez Faire.* Richmond, GB: Hogarth
Press.

Klearman, S. J. (2007, November 26). *Fallon Nevada's Arsenic
Problem.* Retrieved October 5, 2013, from The Legal
Examiner: http://reno.legalexaminer.com/wrongful-
death/fallon-nevadas-arsenic-problem/

Litow, M. M. (2013, February 26). *Bad Medicaid Program Gets Worse
Under ObamaCare.* Retrieved May 23, 2013, from Investor's
Daily: http://news.investors.com/ibd-editorials-
viewpoint/022613-645817-medicaid-still-out-of-control-despite-
obamacare.htm

Locke, J. (1690). *Second Treatise of Government.* London: A Public
Domain Book .

Locke, J. (2011, p. 3). *Second Treatise of Government.* Kindle Edition.

Manmohan S. Kumar, J. W. (2010, July). *Public Debt and Growth.*
Retrieved March 22, 2013, from International Monetary Fund:
http://www.imf.org/external/pubs/cat/longres.cfm?sk=24080.0

Marx, K. (2005, January 25). *The Communist Manifesto (Kindle
Locations 9-12.* Retrieved March 10, 2013, from

www.amazon.com: http://www.amazon.com/kindle-store/dp/B000FC27TA

Mises, L. v. (1944). *Bureacracy, Section 3, p. 1.* Kindle Edition.

Moeller, P. (2013). *Top Ten Corporate Tax Breaks.* Retrieved October 6, 2013, from US News: Deductions are allowed equal to a portion of taxable income attributable to domestic production.

Murray, C. (2012, January 12). *The New American Divide.* Retrieved May 11, 2013, from Wall Street Journal: http://online.wsj.com/article/SB100014240529702043014045 77170733817181646.html

National Center for Education Statistics. (2013). *Fast Faces.* Retrieved May 11, 2013, from Institute of Education Sciences: http://nces.ed.gov/fastfacts/display.asp?id=66

Needham, V. (2013, January 29). *US Debt Headed Toward 200 Percent Of GDP Even After 'Fiscal Cliff' Deal.* Retrieved April 13, 2013, from The Hill: http://thehill.com/blogs/on-the-money/economy/279857-report-fiscal-outlook-not-improved-by-debt-deal#ixzz2JOAYHF2u

Noonan, P. (2012, April 6). *A Stateman's Friendly Advice.* Retrieved April 29, 2013, from Wall Street Joiurnal: http://online.wsj.com/article/SB100014241278873241009045 78402970077475626.html

Novac, J. (2011, January 5). *Tax Waste: 6.1 Billion Hours Spent Complying with Federal Tax Code.* Retrieved September 21, 2013, from Forbes: http://www.forbes.com/sites/janetnovack/2011/01/05/tax-waste-6-1-billion-hours-spent-complying-with-federal-tax-code/

Obama, B. (2012, January 22). *Remarks by the President in the State of the Union.* Retrieved April 22, 2013, from www.whitehouse.gov: http://www.whitehouse.gov/the-press-office/2012/01/24/remarks-president-state-union-address

Obama, B. (2013, September 18). *Obama: 'Raising the Debt Ceiling...Does Not Increase Our Debt,' Though It Has 'Over 100 Times'.* Retrieved September 20, 2013, from CNS News: http://cnsnews.com/mrctv-blog/craig-bannister/obama-raising-debt-ceilingdoes-not-increase-our-debt-though-it-has-over

Office of Management and Budget. (2012). *203 Draft Report to Congress on the Benefits and Costs of Federal Regulation.* Retrieved October 6, 2013, from www.whitehouse.gov: http://www.whitehouse.gov/sites/default/files/omb/inforeg/2013_cb/draft_2013_cost_benefit_report.pdf

Pozen, R. (2013, September 12). How to Create Another Housing Crisis. *Wall Street Journal.* New York, New York, US: Wall Street Journal.

President, O. o. (2009, May). *Estimates Of Job Creation From The American Recovery And Reinvestment Act Of 2009.* Retrieved April 13, 2013, from Council of Economic Advisors: Http://Www.Cg.Sc.Gov/Stimulusguidanceandreports/Documents/05-11-2009-Memo.Pdf

Pullella, P. (2013, October 3). *Pope, in Assisi, calls on Church to shun vanity.* Retrieved October 3, 2013, from Reuters: http://www.reuters.com/article/2013/10/04/us-pope-assisi-idUSBRE9930C720131004

Rasmiussen Reports. (2013, August 07). *Right Direction or Wrong Track.* Retrieved August 10, 2013, from Rasmussen Reports: http://www.rasmussenreports.com/public_content/politics/mood_of_america/right_direction_or_wrong_track

Representatives, H. o. (2009, October 29). *Patient Protection and Affordable Health Care Act.* Retrieved May 22, 2013, from US House of Representatives: http://housedocs.house.gov/rules/health/111_ahcaa.pdf

Research, N. B. (2013, September 13). The Effect of Education on Health. Washington , DC, US.

Richardo, D. (2011, Locations 940-945). *On The Principles of Political Economy, and Taxation.* Kindle Edition.

Roberts, J. (2012, June 29). *Obama's Burdensome Victory.* Retrieved February 7, 2013, from Fox News: http://www.foxnews.com/politics/2012/06/29/obamas-burdensome-victory/

Robespierre, M. (1794, February 5). *Republic of Virtue.* Retrieved December 8, 20122

Robespierre, M. (1794, February 5). *Robispierre, "On Political Morality.* Retrieved August 1, 2013, from George Mason University: http://chnm.gmu.edu/revolution/d/413/

Rousseau, J.-J. (1762). *The Social Contract.* Amsterdam: Available Amazon.

Roy, A. (2012, September 12). *CBO: 11 Million Uninsured Americans Will Be Subject to Obamacare's Individual Mandate 'Penalty Tax'.* Retrieved April 19, 2013, from www.forbes.com: http://www.forbes.com/sites/aroy/2012/09/20/cbo-11-million-uninsured-americans-will-be-subject-to-obamacares-individual-mandate-penalty-tax/

Roy, A. (2013, September 4). *Interactive Map: In 13 States Plus DC Obamacare Will Increase Health Premiums by 24% on Average.* Retrieved September 14, 2013, from www.forbes.com: http://www.forbes.com/sites/theapothecary/2013/09/04/interactive-map-in-13-states-plus-d-c-individual-health-premiums-will-increase-by-an-average-of-24/

Sarbanes-Oxley. (n.d.). Services Outside The Scope Of Practice Of Auditors. *HR 3763* (p. Section 201). Washington D.C.: Library of Congress.

Schmitz, J. (2012, September 11). *New and Larger Costs of Monopoly and Tariffs.* Retrieved January 7, 2013, from Federal Reserve Bank of Minnesota:

http://www.minneapolisfed.org/publications_papers/pub_displa y.cfm?id=4944

Schultz, N. (2011, August 25). *Steve Jobs: America's Greatest Failiure.* Retrieved September 22, 2013, from National Review: http://www.nationalreview.com/articles/275528/steve-jobs-america-s-greatest-failure-nick-schulz

Schumpeter, J. (1942). *Capitalism, Socialism and Democracy.* London and New York: Routledge.

Small Businesss for Sensible Regulations. (2013). *Quick Facts.* Retrieved October 6, 2013, from Small Business for Sensible Regulations: http://www.sensibleregulations.org/resources/facts-and-figures/

Social Security Administration. (2007, October). *Trends in Mortality Differentials and Life Expectancy for Male Social Security–Covered Workers, by Average Relative Earnings.* Retrieved June 10, 2013, from Social Security Administration: http://www.ssa.gov/policy/docs/workingpapers/wp108.html

Soto, H. d. (2000, p. 10). *The Mystery of Captal.* Black Swan Books.

Soto, H. d. (2000, p. 4). *The Mystery of Capital.* Black Swan Books.

Standford Design Thinking College. (2013). *Our Way of Working.* Retrieved April 28, 2013, from Stanford University: http://dschool.stanford.edu/our-point-of-view/#design-thinking

Star, P. (2013, September 10). *Obamacare Regulations Are 8 Times Longer Than Bible.* Retrieved September 21, 2013, from CNS News: http://cnsnews.com/news/article/penny-starr/obamacare-regulations-are-8-times-longer-bible

Strong, J. (2013, June 13). *Ron Johnson's Transformative Proposal.* Retrieved September 1, 2013, from www.nationalreivew.com: http://www.nationalreview.com/article/350983/ron-johnsons-transformative-proposal-jonathan-strong

The Daily Bail. (2012, October 1). *Obamacare Complicated? Check Out The Flow Chart* . Retrieved March 24, 2013, from The Daily Bail: http://dailybail.com/home/obamacare-complicated-check-out-the-flow-chart.html

The Kaiser Family Foundation. (2012, November). *Premiums, Cost-Sharing and Coverage at Public, Private and Non-Profit Employers, A view from the 2012 Employer Health Benefit Survey.* Retrieved June 3, 2013, from Kaiser Family Foundation: http://www.kff.org/insurance/snapshot/chcm112012oth.cfm

Tocqueville, A. d. (2012). *Democracy in American - Volume 1 (p. 195).* Kindle Edition.

Tomsho, R. (2009, August 22). *Study Tallies Education Gap's Effect on GDP.* Retrieved March 22, 2013, from Wall Street Journal: http://online.wsj.com/article/SB124040633530943487.html

Twitchy Staff. (2013, October 1). *Surprise! Obamacare health insruance exchange websites don't wor; Healthcare.gov a total mess.* Retrieved October 1, 2013, from Twitchy US Politics: http://twitchy.com/2013/10/01/surprise-obamacare-health-insurance-exchange-websites-dont-work/

Wall Street Journal. (2013, October 3). IRS Business Protection Act. *Wall Street Journal*, p. A12.

Wilson, W. (1904, November 20). *20th Century Quotes on Constitutional Liimits.* Retrieved May 15, 2013, from Intellectual Takeout: http://www.intellectualtakeout.org/content/20th-century-quotes-constitutional-limits

Wilson, W. (1908). *Constitution Government in the United States.* New York: Columbia University Press.

Wingfield, B. (2013, September 23). *U.S. Solar ground Offers Peace Plan to Avert Trade War.* Retrieved September 28, 2013, from Bloomberg: http://www.bloomberg.com/news/2013-09-23/u-s-solar-group-offers-peace-plan-to-avert-trade-war.html

Xiaohui Gao, J. R. (2013, April 3). Where Have All the IPOs Gone. *Social Science Research Network*, p. Abstract.